DATE DUE

1207.11	Ramona Zamora		

DEMCO

RAISING THE YOUNG BLIND CHILD

RAISING THE YOUNG BLIND CHILD

A Guide for Parents and Educators

Shulamith Kastein
Isabelle Spaulding
Battia Scharf

The Lighthouse,
The New York Association for the Blind, New York

HUMAN SCIENCES PRESS
72 Fifth Avenue   3 Henrietta Street
NEW YORK, NY 10011 ● LONDON, WC2E 8LU

Photographs and drawings by Pat McKee, with the exception of Figures 6-1, 6-2, 16-1, 16-2, and 16-3, which are courtesy of The Lighthouse, The New York Association for the Blind.

Printed in the United States of America
0 987654321

Library of Congress Cataloging in Publication Data

Kastein, Shulamith.
   Raising the young blind child.

   Includes index.
   1. Children, Blind. 2. Child development.
3. Children—Management. I. Spaulding, Isabelle,
joint author. II. Scharf, Battia, joint author.
III. Title.
HV1598.K37   649'.15'11 LC79-17820
ISBN 0-87705-422-3

One sees well only with the heart.
The essential is invisible to the eye.

—*Robert Frost*

CONTENTS

Acknowledgments 13

Foreword 15

Preface 19

Introduction 23

PART I

THE INFANT:

FROM BIRTH TO TWENTY-TWO MONTHS

Chapter 1. LANGUAGE 31

Chapter 2. EARLY MOTOR DEVELOPMENT 37

Early Stimulation 37

Grasping 40

Reaching 41

Rolling Over 42

Sitting 43

Crawling and Creeping 46

Walking Independently   48
Fine Motor Development   51

Chapter 3.   SOCIAL DEVELOPMENT   52

Feeding   52
Drinking from a Cup   56
Finger-feeding   57
Spoon Feeding   58
First Steps in Dressing and Undressing   60

Chapter 4.   EMOTIONAL DEVELOPMENT   61

Separation   61
Social Development   62

Chapter 5.   THE SENSES   65

Hearing   65
Touch   68
Smell   71
Sleep   72

Chapter 6.   PLAY   74

Chapter 7.   BLINDISMS AND MANNERISMS   86

PART II.

THE TODDLER:

FROM TWENTY-THREE MONTHS TO THREE YEARS

Chapter 8. THE BODY   91

    Mobility   91
    Body Concept   96
    Running   96
    Swimming   97
    Fine Motor Development   99

Chapter 9. SENSORY DEVELOPMENT   101

    Hearing   101
    Language   102
    Touch   107
    Smell   108
    Severly Limited Vision   109

Chapter 10. TOWARD INDEPENDENCE   111

    Mealtimes   111
    Toilet Training   113
    Social Development   118
    Emotional Development   120
    Self-Care Skills   122

Chapter 11. PLAY   128

PART III.
THE YOUNG CHILD:
FROM THREE TO FIVE YEARS

Chapter 12. LANGUAGE 141

Chapter 13. ADVANCED MOTOR DEVELOPMENT 144

Gross Motor Development, Mobility, and
Orientation 144
Trailing 150
Sighted-Guide Technique 153
Fine Motor Development 154

Chapter 14. GROWING UP 156

Grooming 156
Dressing and Undressing 157
Mealtimes 160
Helping Around the House 163

Chapter 15. PRE-READING 165

Pre-Braille 165
Tactile Discrimination 168
Counting 173
Auditory Discrimination 176

Chapter 16. LEARNING THROUGH PLAY 179

Chapter 17. FIRST AWARENSS OF BLINDNESS 189

Chapter 18.   MULTIPLE IMPAIRMENTS   194

Letter to a Mother   197
Suggested Readings   198
Index   199

ACKNOWLEDGMENTS

We wish to express our gratitude to the administration of The New York Association for the Blind for their encouragement and support and to the staff of the Child Development Center for sharing their observations with us. We are grateful to colleagues and parents for their interest, their generous advice and fruitful criticisms. Most of all we want to thank the parents for their trust and shared experiences and the children for what they have taught us.

SHULAMITH KASTEIN
ISABELLE SPAULDING
BATTIA SCHARF

FOREWORD

Parents of children born with severe visual impairment need help and support with the task of raising their child. This book shares with parents of visually impaired children, the observations and suggestions of the authors based on their long experience in the New York Lighthouse (The New York Association for the Blind) Child Development Center.

The present Child Development Center represents the growth and development of services for visually impaired children and their families since 1925 when the Lighthouse Nursery School was established. Programs for children have been modified and expanded to meet the changing needs of those seeking assistance from the agency.

In the 1950s, mental health consultants were used to assess and prescribe for those children who exhibited behavioral symptoms. The increased number of multi-handicapped children following the rubella epidemic of 1964 further demonstrated the need for a coordinated, integrated diagnostic and therapeutic program. The agency staff, including consultants, was broadened to include specialists in psychiatry, language, hearing, and special education in addition to the ophthalmologist, pediatrician, psychologist, and social worker already seeing the child and family. This amplification of the program was recognized as a new orientation in our services for visually impaired

15

preschool children and was renamed the Child Development Center for Blind and Visually Impaired Children.

The Center adheres to the principle that the visually impaired child belongs with his nonimpaired peers in community education programs. But before the child and his family are ready for a community experience much preparatory work is necessary. The major part of this work occurs in the home. The authors aim to encourage parents, who now face the problems of bringing up a visually impaired child, to think through the problems encountered by the child at each stage of development. They seek to do this by offering their observations of how visually impaired children grow and how the parents can help the child cope with each developmental milestone.

There are resources available in communities across the country to support parents by offering professional help in assessment, counseling, and additional intervention. (See Appendix for resource information and suggested readings.) It is significant that this book begins and ends with statements about parents rather than about children. The preface is a statement of the emotional reactions of parents to the knowledge of the child's impairment. Parents must deal with the grief and disappointment of the discovery of the child's impairment before being able to work at nurturing the child. The impaired child requires more time, effort, and patience than the physically intact child. Autobiographical accounts of visually impaired children's experiences while growing up acknowledge the importance that their parents have had for them and the unique relationship between parent and child. This book also recognizes in its final chapter the child's mother who, for the most part, must carry the daily burdens of caring for the preschool child.

The Administration of The New York Association for the Blind has encouraged the development of this book from its inception. We hope that it is of help to all parents faced with the task of bringing up a visually impaired child and that the recognition of shared rather than unique problems will make the task easier. This book offers suggestions rather than rules.

ARLENE R. GORDON, M.A.
Associate Executive Director
The New York Association for the Blind

ARTHUR E. GILLMAN, M.D.
Director of Research Development
The New York Association for the Blind

PREFACE

No parent is ever prepared for the advent of a blind child. Such a diagnosis places the family in crisis. A family's initial reaction to having a visually handicapped child has a singular theme—loss, mourning, and grief. This reaction is related to the psychological preparation for a new child that occurs during pregnancy and involves the wish and expectation for a perfect child. The mourning process, then, is actually a reaction to the loss of a healthy child. The overwhelming aspect of this situation is that there is little time for grieving. The parents feel a demand to invest in the blind child. This pressure can stem from others in their environment or arise from their own feelings of guilt. In addition, the reality of the needs of the new child allow parents little time or energy for the mourning process. Consequently, it is not uncommon for a parent in this situation to temporarily retreat from these demands. Some parents have excessive needs for sleep during this initial period while others become extremely involved in activities outside the home. It is important to realize that this is a period of upheaval in family life.

The discrepancy between the anticipated perfect child and the reality of the blind child represents a family crisis. It has been said that the stability of the family and that of its members hinges on a delicate pattern of emotional balance and interchange. The behavior of each member is affected by every other. The advent of a handicapped child into a family upsets the equilibrium of family life; this in turn can affect the progress and adjustment of the child.

There are varied reactions to this crisis. Some parents grow closer to one another while others move apart. If there is mutual blame and recrimination, one sees the development of excessive and unusually intense feelings of guilt and personal inadequacy. This often places a strain on the husband-wife relationship. Parents are initially so emotionally drained that they are unable to give to each other or to their other children. The birth of a healthy infant into a family creates adjustment problems for all. Having an exceptional child places exceptional demands upon families. It can be assumed that whatever the effect, the family changes and probably cannot be reconstructed as it was before the arrival of the blind child.

Parents are never pleased to learn that they have produced a handicapped child. Consequently, it is not unusual for parents to feel angry. This anger is expressed in different ways by families. Some parents direct their anger at the doctors or hospitals who have an involvement with the child. They express this anger by looking for service elsewhere. It is not uncommon for parents to feel anger toward friends and acquaintances who have healthy children. In some cases, the anger they feel toward the handicapped child is acted out on the healthy child. It is not unusual to see such parents overreact verbally and physically to this child for minor infractions, such as accidentally spilling a glass of milk. The parent is usually confused by such actions and feels guilty. Parents need to be reassured that it is acceptable and common to have feelings of anger related not only to having a blind child but also toward the child himself. When these feelings are understood, the parent's need to displace anger on the healthy child is usually diminished.

Some families tend to disengage themselves from community relationships when they have a blind child. Consequently, they experience themselves as isolated, devaluated, and socially estranged. This can manifest itself in feelings of hostility toward the child who is seen as the cause of their social isolation. This situation is usually the result of the child being viewed as frustrating the family aims and aspirations. In these families, the blind youngster is often pushed for unrealistic achievement levels so that the "family image" can be maintained.

Child care and long-term dependency concerns are concrete and realistic problems presented by many parents, particularly those who are financially burdened. Time demands on parents are greatly increased in families where household help is not affordable. As we all know, excess long-standing fatigue places a strain on any family life. Parents are urged to seek child care help from community agencies, religious organizations, and volunteer bureaus in their area. It is critical that parents be able to have some time away from the home environment unburdened by children, as well as relief in the home. The parents' feelings that surface when a blind child enters the family system affect the growth experience of that child. These children tend to experience different parenting than that of the so-called "normal" child. Until now, there have been few guidebooks available for parents and none as comprehensive as *Raising the Young Blind Child*. Parents have been accused of overprotection or infantilizing their child. The reality of the situation is such that there is difficulty in knowing how much protection the child requires. Most parents need some professional guidance in order to determine realistic limitations for this child. When this is given, parents are usually willing to allow the child the freedom necessary for normal development.

It is important for parents to understand and accept a child's limitations. If parents have confused expectations for the blind child, a push-pull struggle ensues between parent and child. This is characterized by alternating periods of expecting too much and then giving up in despair. One effect of this is to increase the child's negativism. It is essential for parents to come to terms with the reality of the child's handicap in order to make decisions and provide the support that will enable him to lead a healthy and productive life. As in any life problem, a blind child will call forth his parents' characteristic and individual ways of functioning. The better the parents are able to understand their own feelings and to act upon that understanding, the better they will be able to relate to the child and the problem of his handicap.

RUTH BROOKS, M.S.W.

The New York Association for the Blind

INTRODUCTION

Visitors to the Child Development Center at The Lighthouse, a nursery school for blind and visually impaired children, are often amazed that the classrooms look very much like those in any preschool setting, with the same or similar equipment and with children smiling, laughing, talking, romping, and engaging in activities very much like sighted children their age. Some visitors are also surprised to see children wearing eyeglasses. The definition of legal blindness encompasses a wide range of visual capability from total absence of vision to sufficient vision to enable the child to read regular print. Children who are classified legally blind may thus function very much like sighted children. In this book, we are addressing ourselves to the parents of children who are totally blind or who have extremely limited vision, so limited they will probably require braille as one of their methods of reading and writing.

The blind child never ceases to amaze us: he can demonstrate the same curiosity about and involvement in the world around him, the same joy in discovery as does the sighted child.* The blind three year old who can role play, imitate, and "make believe" like his sighted playmate shows

---

*The use of the masculine pronoun throughout the text is purely conventional; the reader should be aware that when it is used, it is meant to include females as well.

us that he has successfully mastered some of the developmental hazards of his visual deficit. To describe how the parents and other members of the family can help the blind child achieve complete mastery is the purpose of this book.

Blind children can and do grow up to be productive, independent, self-fulfilled individuals who enjoy life, if they live in an environment that provides adequate stimulation for human relationships and emotional and intellectual growth.

Although the concepts concerning handicapped children (and adults) have undergone considerable change in recent years, some archaic ideas still exist. In order to ensure the child's normal development, both parents and professionals may have to change their attitudes to help him. This help is needed most during the first years of life, the time when the basis for all his future experience and learning is formed. His needs as a child, and his special needs as a blind child, must be understood not only by the parents but by all the people in the child's environment. From the moment a visual deficit is suspected or diagnosed, most of what the child cannot see will have to be made accessible to him through his other senses. For instance, it is the parents' voices and words that will have to indicate and assure the child of their presence. Body contact and the sensation of touch will have to lead the child to the awareness of his own and his parents' bodies, and later to awareness of his physical environment, by taking him to feel what is around him or by bringing to him what he would see if he could. In this way, by touching, feeling, and listening, his curiosity will be aroused and his desire to explore awakened. This is the basis for the emergence of the person, the unfolding of the intellect.

The children at the Child Development Center taught us that in a group of blind children, each is as different from the other as any child is in a group. Observing blind children, we also learned that most of them find their own way to circumvent their lack of vision, and develop their own style of learning. This discovery helped us in turn to provide assistance and offer suggestions to the parents of children who failed to do this on their own, and to offer alternatives to fit their needs. For instance, one child would use his entire body to obtain information he could not adequately obtain through the mere touch of his hands. Another child would find his mouth a more reliable source of information about objects in his environment, and another his forehead or cheek. Each child seemed to develop a preference for utilizing a particular area of his body. In the very early stages of development, these spontaneous attempts should be encouraged. They are dropped by the child when he acquires other means of exploration, especially language. Language will remain the major source of acquiring knowledge, of "seeing" the world, of communicating with others as well as with himself.

Among handicapping conditions in children, blindness has been studied the least and its effect on the development of the child and what intervention is necessary are still not fully explored. The need for information on blind infants and children, which has been expressed in numerous requests from parents and professional workers from all over the United States and abroad, persuaded us to share our experience and observations and to use our successes and failures as guidelines for parents who have the long and arduous but deeply rewarding task of raising a blind child.

There are many different causes for impaired vision or blindness and a number of ways in which the condition manifests itself, as well as various ages at which it first occurs. Although an infant may appear to be blind and the parents may have been told the child is blind, the amount of functional vision cannot always be determined at an early age. Moreover, treatment such as surgery may improve or restore vision in some cases, while other conditions may cause progressive deterioration. It is important for the parents to work with the ophthalmologist, since the parents have more opportunities to observe the child's reaction to light such as blinking when exposed to sunlight or when a light in a dark room is switched on; they may notice the child following a moving object with his eyes or reaching for objects unexpectedly, without groping. If any of these observations are made, they should be brought immediately to the ophthalmologist's attention. On the other hand, if a child who is considered to have normal vision does not seem to react to visual stimulation or fails to follow people with his eyes, or if the parent observes anything unusual in the child's eyes or visual behavior, the pediatrician should immediately be consulted so that referral to an eye specialist can be made if indicated.

When impaired vision or blindness is detected or confirmed, the parents experience a profound emotional shock. Although it is always painful to know that one's child is impaired in any way, visual impairment, especially blindness, is often devastating. The parents are now faced not only with the normal apprehensions about raising a child, but with problems for which they are totally unprepared.

During this period of sorrow when parents need help most, they are sometimes reluctant to seek it and often are least receptive to outside intervention. Parents differ, of course, in their emotional strengths and weaknesses, and their reactions differ. Because of the shattering impact of discovering one's child is blind, it may take the parents some time to face reality, and they are often unable to discuss the problem even with members of their own extended families. Communication is crucial, since the parents need help in accepting their child's impairment and since their attitude toward the child is in jeopardy; parents may become preoccupied with the impairment and forget the child.

Parents who have raised other children often feel inadequate when faced with a blind child. A common statement often heard from parents is "I just did not know what to do."

The concept of blindness is frightening to most people because many misconceptions surround the condition. Parents do not know what to expect of a blind child or his future. What they need to know when they first find out their child is blind is that he can grow and develop into a well-functioning and productive human being. This information is most effective when it is conveyed to the parents by someone who has experienced raising a blind child. We have frequently heard the mother of an older child say to the mother of a blind infant "You won't cry when you see what he can do." Although it is often difficult to change parents' attitudes simply by having them read about others in their position, they must be made aware that it is they who set the emotional tone in the home. It is important that the child be treated like his siblings, that he be given an appropriate degree of responsibility, and that he be fully accepted as a respected family member. As with a sighted child, the goal of the parent should be to help the blind child become as independent as possible; only then can he develop feelings of self-worth.

Our intention is not to minimize the depth of the experience or the seriousness of the condition, but to bring it into perspective for the sake of the child and the parents. We also want to stress that blind children, like all children, need a healthy parent-child relationship in order to develop normally. Any interference in the relationship may deter growth, just as it would in any other child. In addition, the blind child needs parent intervention in order to help him understand and integrate what he hears, touches, and smells. Our purpose is to help parents of young blind children to know not only how the blind child "sees" the world, but when and how intervention is necessary.

Since the blind child develops in almost the same way as

the sighted child, we will follow the same sequential steps in this book that occur in the development of the sighted child, allowing, of course, for differences in individual children. Most parents are aware that each child develops at his own rate, some taking longer to reach the next developmental stage than others. Some children either skip a step or reverse the order, standing before sitting, for example. Blind children may take a different route, too, but parents need not be concerned unless a markedly deviant pattern is observed. Since each child is unique, parents should refrain from comparing their child with others of the same age. We deliberately do not give specific ages for each developmental step. Rather, we follow the development of the sighted child, allowing for a somewhat different rate of growth. We hope that each parent will determine the developmental level his child has reached and help him toward the next step, regardless of the child's age.

Since the development of the blind child follows a course similar to that taken by a sighted child, we suggest that parents of blind children read this book as an adjunct to their particular favorite book on child care or child development. We also hope to convey to parents of blind children that their blind child is a child first, a child who just happens to be blind. He has the same needs as any other child. But parents of blind children are vulnerable, and they tend to focus on the blindness rather than on the child. One mother considered the turning point in acquiring a more positive attitude toward her blind child to be the words of a staff member who suggested: "Try to forget your child is blind and enjoy him."

Part I

THE INFANT:
FROM BIRTH TO TWENTY-TWO
MONTHS

hands and feet—nor will he know they exist, unless he can experience them through touch, sound, or taste. In other words, he will not be motivated to explore, unless guided to what he cannot see, unless made to feel and hear what is brought to him. By the same token, if there is no awareness of the environment, there is no desire or need to communicate. Yet the means to communicate not only with his environment but with himself—language—will have to be the link, the interpretor, and the means to open the road to form mental concepts, to become aware of and learn about the world, himself, and life. This places an additional burden on the parents of the child, although at the same time it holds very special joy and rewards for them.

From the earliest stages, the parents have to bear in mind what the child misses through his lack of vision: facial expressions, body movements, the awareness of someone's presence in the room. People and objects exist for the blind child only through touch and sound. The blind child will turn to the source of sound, although it may take him longer to do so than it does the sighted child since he cannot see where the sound comes from. It will also take him longer to learn to relate a sound to its source, since he does not have the visual image to help him. Touch, and later verbal description, must be afforded him so he can learn to listen to where the object goes when it falls, to experience and judge distances and location by sound alone. In order to do this, his body has to be kept in touch with the moving object so he can experience its path and movement, location, and distance. This can easily be done by letting him hear a toy car roll across the table, and immediately afterward letting him hold the car as it follows the same path; by dropping a block and then lifting the child down to follow the block and find it. These activities will teach him what the sighted child learns by watching: that objects do not disappear into a void; that they go somewhere and remain there, to be found again and retrieved. The blind child must learn that these facts are true not only for objects, but even more important, that they apply to his parents, whose presence he seeks and needs. Again, they must remember that the child cannot see them and that his eyes cannot follow them; that he must hear their voices, the sound of their activities, and their footsteps to know whether they are nearby or far away. Each member of the household will have to learn to identify himself when he enters the room, to use his voice and allow noises of his activities to maintain contact with the child who cannot see him.

The blind child smiles, laughs, cries, and vocalizes (babbles) just as does the sighted infant, and will begin to repeat sounds and words at almost the same time as the sighted child. Because he cannot see his parents' facial movements as they speak, the child should be encouraged, in a playful way, to explore their faces, their mouths, their cheeks. Since he cannot see them smile or frown when they express happiness or sadness as the sighted child can, the parents must always be aware that their voices must convey these feelings to the child.

As the child becomes aware of and then familiar with people and objects in his environment, he will, by touch, sound, and smell, be able to form concepts of what he cannot see but can hear and touch. He will learn to recognize the voices of members of the family and differentiate them from the voices of strangers. He will recognize and identify the footsteps of the people around him. (It is therefore a good idea to leave the floor bare.) He will know by touch the thing that is a spoon and soon learn that it is to eat with, that the cup is to drink from, that the brush and comb are for the hair. He is developing concepts of people and of objects, and of some of the uses of objects. During this time, the blind child, more than the sighted child, needs to be exposed to language. Whatever he touches should be named, whatever he does or whatever is done for him should be described in the appropriate words—not in a string of sentences, but simply in the words that clearly refer to what is occurring. As soon as the child learns the names of objects and actions, he has another means to help him conceptualize them. Here too, the lack of vision will make it more difficult to give the word meaning, to connect word and object, since there is no visual image to reinforce the relation. The inborn capacity for the development of language will soon enable the child to know the meaning of a word even without having the object present. When we realize that the child has to arrive at this step without the reference of the visual image, without being able to perceive the "whole" at a glance, we can appreciate the enormity of the task and the marvelous functions of the brain. In order to facilitate this process of concept formation and to parallel the development and experience of the sighted child, we have found the "object basket" most helpful. This is a collection of common objects, such as a brush, comb, cup, keys, etc. placed in a basket which the blind child can explore, just as a sighted child looks at pictures in a book. The objects can be changed from time to time. As the child becomes older, more complex objects can be included.

We have observed that during the period from 12 to about 22 months, the progression in comprehension of spoken language and the expressive speech of the blind child often slows down. It seems that this period in a child's development is dominated by visual experience and the blind child therefore is at a disadvantage, needing additional time to reach the next developmental milestone. By 18 to 22 months the blind child if offered experiences similar to those of the sighted child will show that he has not lost any skills; he has just taken a little longer to develop them. He will now respond to spoken questions and commands, will begin to use words to name, to request, and to refuse. He will begin to communicate verbally. Since this is also the period in which he begins to walk, and his field of experience is therefore expanding, it is essential that he be supplied the words for his newly acquired experiences.

It is necessary to replace the visual attraction and the awareness of presence by sight during these months with sound and touch to let the baby know what he cannot see. For instance, objects, preferably those that make a sound or noise, should be placed in his hands or so close that he will touch them with some part of his body.

Since he cannot see his body, he will not be guided by sight to touch and play with it. He has to be encouraged to "find" his feet, his hands, etc. Here, too, naming parts of his body as they are touched will help him form the appropriate concepts. It is not enough to ask "Where is your nose?" He has never seen his own reflection or anybody else's. He can know only by touch the parts of the body named.

In the development of language, interaction plays a major role, especially for the blind child, since he misses the permanent reference—the visual image—of the word; the spoon, the ball, even his own feet vanish when touch is lost or the sound stopped. The child who finds objects in the same place will learn to navigate better and sooner than the child who has to search in different places each time he hears the word. When he begins to sit in a highchair, the word "up" will remain meaningless unless he is physically experiencing the movement while the word is being uttered. The concrete experience of the meaning of words is the beginning of language development in all children. Parents should continue to use their voices as they move away from the child into another room, or move the child away while someone is speaking so that he can experience the difference in the loudness as it changes with distance. Later, he will use sound as a measure for distance.

Articulation of speech sounds depends not only on hearing the sounds and words as they are produced by others and oneself, but also requires precise and rapid movements of the tongue, lips, and jaws. It is essential that these muscles be ready when the child begins to use them for speech. The same muscles are used for chewing food, and the chewing of solid, and especially crisp, foods will provide the necessary preparation. This should be borne in mind when solid food is introduced, and the baby shows resistance to it, as is often the case.

Communication is a two-way system: We have to be able to understand what others say, and we have to be able to express our own thoughts, feelings, and desires through words. In either the sighted or the blind child, one or both of these systems of communication may be disturbed. Since the blind child relies to a considerable extent on language as a substitute for vision, it is all the more important to promote his language development. And since hearing plays a dominant role in verbal language, the child's hearing should be investigated.

Most children begin to talk by repeating words, practicing in a playful way and enjoying their newly acquired skill. Often they will do this to determine the effect of an utterance once they attach some meaning to it. They have found a means to control their environment, and relish it, having taken another step toward independence, provided their efforts are appropriately met by the adult.

To facilitate the understanding and use of spoken language, it is important not only to name people, objects, or actions to which the child is exposed, but to establish a routine of presenting the same objects during feeding, dressing, bathing, etc., to the child so that the tactile (touching), the auditory (sound making), and the olfactory (smell) experiences remain the same and are therefore easier to remember. As soon as a child has learned the meaning of a word, for example, a spoon, and he can "find" the spoon among two or three objects in front of him, a variety of spoons can be introduced and he will quickly learn that they are all "spoons." At about this time, he may be able to repeat the word after the parent and will soon do so without prompting when given a spoon to hold, or spontaneously when he wants one—the start of verbal communication.

Chapter 2

EARLY MOTOR DEVELOPMENT

EARLY STIMULATION

When blindness is recognized at or soon after birth, the parents of a blind baby must bear in mind that their child must use other senses, as limited as they may be at the very beginning, to ascertain facial expressions, movements of people and objects, the bottle or breast, etc. The fact that the baby cannot see may often tempt the parents to do less for and with him, less touching, less talking, less cuddling, when he needs not only what the sighted baby does, but much more. At every opportunity, especially at feeding time, the parents should make a conscious effort to put the baby's hand on their faces, to move the baby's face or their own close enough to be touched, placing his hands on the mother's breast or on the bottle. Making sounds, singing, and talking to the baby is another necessary means of making him aware of her presence. By introducing the feeding with the same sounds or words each time, allowing the baby to hear the shaking of the bottle or feel its warmth, the parent will teach the infant to seek and use information in the future from listening and touching instead of looking. Soon, he will learn to recognize and distinguish the approach of people by listening to the sound of footsteps, just as the sighted child does by looking. Bare floors, at least in the child's room, will make it easier for the baby to learn this.

Since parents often do not know what to expect from their blind infant, they sometimes become anxious and wonder if the child's development will be normal. It will comfort many parents to know that, provided the infant is appropriately stimulated, he will follow about the same sequence of gross motor development as the sighted child, except perhaps, for some delay in creeping and walking.

The blind baby needs to be placed into different positions just as the sighted baby does. A sighted infant lying on his stomach will attempt to lift his head because he is attracted by what he sees, and in doing so, strengthens the neck muscles. The blind baby has no reason to raise his head when on his stomach, and unless he is stimulated is not likely to do so. Thus it is necessary for the parent to encourage this activity. This can be done by calling the infant from a point just above his head or attracting him with a favorite sound-making object, and at the same time raising his chin. When he does raise his head, he should be rewarded by placing the object into his hand.

In the early months, many parents of sighted infants exercise their babies in order to stimulate motor activity. Encouraging the blind baby to move is even more important, because the baby is less motivated to move, since the environment is not attracting him visually. In addition to strengthening body muscles, exercise is a pleasant way for the parent to interact with the infant in a playful but purposeful manner. In the examples of exercises that follow, we found the most comfortable position was placing the baby on his back on a blanket, either on the floor or on a table. Each exercise should be done several times.

Knee bends
Hold the baby's legs straight just above the ankles; bend his knees over his chest, then return them to a straight position. An alternative is to hold the baby's legs near the ankles, bend one knee up toward his chest while keeping the other straight. Alternate the movement. The baby will love the exercise when it is speeded up. Next, bend the infants legs up and outward toward his chest holding them at the knees. Spread his legs apart to the sides of his body as far as they can go without discomfort.

Arms and shoulders
Hold the baby's hands and raise both arms up to the sides of his head, then lower them to his sides. Alternate arms: while one arm is up the other should be at his side. Then, holding his hands, cross his arms over his chest; next, stretch them out to his sides.

Without bending the knee or arm, raise his right arm and right leg up toward his head, as far as it will go without making the baby uncomfortable. Repeat with left side.

The next step is to raise the *right* arm and the *left* leg (without bending arm or leg) up toward his head. Reverse sides, raising *left* arm and *right* leg.

Sit-ups
With the baby on his back, slowly pull him up by his hands to a sitting position, then slowly lower him.

Rolling the baby from side to side taking precautions not to hurt his arms can also be fun.

These are only a few of the many exercises the baby will benefit from and enjoy. The suggested readings list some of the books on the market describing exercises recommended for the sighted baby that may also be used for the blind infant.

In the very early months, all babies' movements are diffuse. As the infant's neuromuscular system develops, he learns how to move discrete parts of his body. The sighted baby has the advantage of seeing these movements; the blind baby can be helped by substituting sound and touch. Therefore, to ensure arm and leg movements that closely correspond with the amount of motor activity in the sighted baby and also to make the baby aware he can control his movements, parents might attach a small bell around the baby's wrist or ankle, making sure it is secure. In the beginning, it helps the infant become aware that movement produces a sound, thus motivating motor activity. Later on, it will help the baby learn how to move only the arm or leg with the bell attached.

GRASPING

Grasping is the ability of the infant to voluntarily hold an object when it is placed in his hand. It is not to be confused with the previous stage of the involuntary reflex grasp that a baby has at birth and which diminishes gradually. Like the sighted baby, the blind baby has no difficulty voluntarily holding an object when it is placed in his hand. Objects should be placed in the infant's hands from time to time during his waking hours so that he becomes aware of his hands and of what they can do. Some babies maintain a clenched fist. If a baby does this, his hand can be relaxed if he is gently patted beginning at his shoulder and working down toward his hand until it opens. When his hand opens, an object can be placed in it.

Around the time the baby learns to grasp, he also learns to bring both hands together to the center of his body, either at the chest or near the face. Later, when he begins to reach, he will begin by reaching with both hands at first and then with only one hand. However, if the blind baby does not bring his hands to the midline of his body, he should be shown how, by bringing them together for him. Doing so adds to greater awareness of his hands. At about the same time the sighted baby begins to discover his hands by gazing at them, the blind baby must feel them. He, too, needs to discover his hands and know he can put them together. Once he becomes aware of his hands, he has to be encouraged to touch his head, face, nose, ears, arms, and legs to discover the rest of his body through his hands.

REACHING

The sighted baby begins to reach after he has learned to grasp because he is visually attracted to objects and is motivated to extend his hand and reach for them. This is not the case with the blind baby. He reaches for objects only after they are brought into contact with his body. While the sighted baby reaches because he sees the concrete and tangible object, the blind baby has to depend on sound, which is abstract and does not yet represent the object. The only way the baby can know an object is present is by touching it. We assume that the reason the blind baby does not reach on sound cue is because he is unable to make the connection between the sound he hears and the object that makes the sound. Obviously, this intellectual conceptualization does not develop until he is older. The sighted baby has vision to provide him with the stimulus that triggers reaching, and can do this without the more advanced conceptual stage in development. We make this point to alert parents and to prevent their disappointment when they shake a rattle or object and the baby fails to respond. He will eventually reach for it when he can make the connection, but he usually will not do so until after he has learned to sit, whereas the sighted baby reaches for objects before, after having studied and followed them with his eyes.

In order to facilitate this association and to minimize the delay, the parent can try to place a favorite rattle or soundmaking toy in both of the baby's hands. After the baby has held it for a few seconds, it should be gently removed.

Standing a few inches away from the baby, the object should be shaken and then placed back into the baby's hands. It might also help to extend the baby's hands toward the object while making the sound, to help develop his awareness that the sound is coming from the object.

ROLLING OVER

Rolling over is the next stage in development. The sighted baby begins to roll, first from his stomach to his back and then from his back to his stomach. Later he learns that this activity helps him move from one place to another. The blind baby is capable of the same movements. However, he is not likely to be motivated to lift his head and track objects and to roll over, and has to be helped to do it. He can be encouraged to roll over by placing him on a padded, flat surface on his stomach, folding his right arm under his chest and gently moving his left shoulder and left hip, turning him onto his back. Repeat the process, rolling him to the other side. Teaching him to roll from his back to his stomach is slightly more difficult, as it is for all babies. Raise his right arm out and upward and with the other hand on his left buttock, give him a gentle push, rolling him over to his stomach. Repeat, pushing him over on the other side. Patting and praising him will encourage him to learn. Rewarding him with his favorite toy may also help. This should be done twice daily when the baby is most relaxed. Once he has learned to roll over, he needs to learn that rolling is a means of locomotion, which will get him from one point to another. He can be helped to understand this by placing a sound making object a short distance away from him, where he will have to roll to it.

After the baby has learned to roll over independently, boundaries the sighted baby has seen all along should be experienced by the blind baby. To find them, the baby needs to roll from side to side in his crib, so that his body comes in contact with the sides, making him aware they exist. As the baby becomes more familiar with his crib, he will be rolling over more and more frequently, and in this way will experience the distance he cannot see.

A playpen is used by parents as a safe place for the baby to play in. For the blind baby, it not only serves this purpose but has another advantage. It is a circumscribed area that is larger than his crib and that, therefore, expands his spatial awareness. The infant will learn that after a certain amount of rolling, he will reach the side of the playpen, thus experiencing a space larger than his crib. Once the baby becomes familiar with the boundaries of his crib and playpen, he may want to stay in them for longer periods than the sighted baby because it affords him the security of a specific area he is familiar with and where all his toys are within reach. They allow the child more freedom of movement compared to the often frightening experience of the void in open spaces. One parent reported that her child moved, pivoted, walked across the crib and was generally more active in her crib and playpen than any other place. This freedom of movement is necessary for the blind child, but parents must remember that once the child has mastered the early skills of gross motor movement he should be encouraged to explore the environment beyond the crib and playpen. Therefore, while the baby may prefer the security of the crib and playpen, it is not wise to keep him in them longer than necessary. He should be ready to move out of the playpen when he is able to creep, stand, and cruise. The only way a blind child learns about his environment is by coming into contact with it.

SITTING

Sitting is the next stage in gross motor development. Some children, whether sighted or blind, do not sit by themselves. If a blind baby fails to sit up, he may need encouragement by being propped up, either in a high chair or in the corner of a couch or an armchair. If he is wobbly, small rolled-up towels can be tucked between his body and the sides of the chair. Keeping the baby occupied with his favorite toys while propped up will lengthen the sitting time.

Another rather unusual, but very effective, way to facilitate and reinforce sitting is the use of a small cardboard box, just large enough for the baby's body to fit into when he is in a sitting position. He will receive added support if his feet can touch the side of the box. Toys or objects can be placed on the baby's lap where he can feel them, pick them up, drop them, and retrieve them. The closeness of the box, in which the objects can fall only to his lap, helps him develop the concept of retrievability and eventually of the permanence of objects.

Sitting the baby in a walker, even before he can sit independently, is another means of promoting sitting. Although walkers are not universally recommended for babies because they encourage easy reach and touching of objects that might be dangerous, the dangers are minimal for the blind child since he will not be attracted to them by sight. The walker can provide the blind baby with the experience of movement, and will give him the opportunity to accidentally discover parts of the environment by bumping into them. It also allows the baby his first independent experience of movement in space. Some blind babies discover a bouncing movement in the walker and often become preoccupied with the bouncing. In such instances, the baby can be shown, by moving his feet forward in an alternate step, how he can move himself. The child will also soon discover how he can stand, at first holding on to the rim of the walker and later standing with just a bit of support from the seat alone. The walker should be used discriminately, since some babies, sighted or blind, grow to depend on the walker for locomotion, and that may delay the onset of independent walking. Three or four times a day in the walker for ten minutes each should be sufficient.

At about this time the sighted baby begins to transfer objects from hand to hand. Soon after, he finds he can bang two blocks together and create a noise. Later he is fascinated when he can turn objects upside down by rotating his wrists. These developmental steps occur so naturally in the sighted baby that parents often overlook them. Although some blind babies discover these manipulations on their own, parents of blind babies need to be aware of these sequential steps so they can help their child attain them. Not only do they make the baby aware of what his hands can do, but they also may facilitate fine motor skills and coordination. The baby can be shown the movement by taking his hands and going through the motion with him.

For the sighted baby, learning to pull up into a standing position is generally a simple accomplishment because he sees the rungs on the crib or playpen and uses them for support to lift himself up. The blind baby is at a disadvantage because he lacks the visual clues to help him, and although some blind babies initiate pulling themselves up and do so around the same time as a sighted baby, some need to be shown how. Placing the baby's hands on the rungs and giving him a boost by slightly pushing his bottom up will give the baby an idea of how he can pull himself up. Once the baby realizes how easily it can be done, he is usually pleased with his new discovery, and often wants it repeated several times. This skill is usually mastered quickly by most blind babies, after they have engaged in it for a few minutes two or three times a day. Placing toys at standing height for the baby in the crib or playpen will give him added pleasure, in addition to making him aware that he can play while standing up. He may have to be shown how to hold on with one hand while playing with the other.

Learning how to get down from a standing position is slightly more difficult, both for the sighted and the blind baby. Many sighted babies become frightened because they cannot find a way to lower their bodies after they have managed to stand up. The blind baby may even be more frightened because he cannot see the distance to the bottom of the crib or playpen. The parent can show him how to bend one knee and slowly move downward while holding on to the rung of the crib or playpen just as the parent of a sighted baby would. With a little practice, all babies learn this step without difficulty.

CRAWLING AND CREEPING

Most babies learn to crawl on their stomachs before they learn to get up on their hands and knees and creep. Some babies learn to walk without ever crawling or creeping. This is also true for the blind baby. However, the blind baby is not likely to creep or crawl at the same age the sighted baby masters this skill, mainly because he does not have the visual attraction to motivate him.

Since crawling or creeping is an extension of reaching, it usually does not develop until after the child has learned to reach on sound cue. Crawling and creeping give the blind baby an opportunity to learn that there is a world around him he cannot see, a world the sighted baby learns a great deal about just by looking, even before he learns to move about. Some blind babies crawl and creep on their own without any adult intervention, as naturally as sighted babies do. However, they are the exceptions rather than the rule. The majority of blind babies need prompting. For example, the parents can wrap a towel around the baby's torso and then lift him slightly so that his hands and knees will just touch the floor. Another way is to position the baby on his hands and knees and give him a slight push on the soles of his feet. A more difficult technique, but one worth trying, is to place the baby on his hands and knees and move his hands and knees forward in an alternate creeping motion. Each of these methods requires that another person attract the baby with the sound of one of his favorite toys while he is being stimulated to move.

Parents may worry that once the baby has learned to creep, he may be more vulnerable to getting hurt. Oddly enough, most blind babies who creep from room to room learn quickly where the obstacles are located after they have experienced a bump or two. Staircases, of course, need to be blocked off, just as they do for a sighted baby.

Occasionally, a baby might be more fearful and become discouraged after the first bruise. One little girl was resourceful enough to creep while holding onto a toy that was about seven inches long, which she kept extended in her hand. When she hit an obstacle she felt it first with the toy rather than with her head, thereby protecting herself.

After a blind baby has learned to stand and feels secure on his feet, he will attempt to cruise. Most sighted babies begin to cruise by holding on to the rim of the crib or playpen and later cruise on the floor holding onto furniture. Blind babies generally have no difficulty learning to cruise in the playpen or crib, although some may need a little help by being shown how they can hold on to the rim for support. However, the blind baby is more relaxed when cruising or walking either in a very familiar place or holding on to a familiar person. Therefore, unless he has had experience in creeping on the floor, he may be frightened of cruising in open space. The sighted baby has little difficulty when he is standing near a piece of furniture and can see the distance to another piece that he can use for support. He is also attracted by objects that motivate him to move from one place to another, and gradually he takes up the challenge of mastering increasingly longer distances. However, the blind baby lacks these incentives to move, and it becomes necessary for the parent to set up an area where the furniture is close together so the baby feels secure in moving. If he is placed, for instance, in a spot where a couch, a coffee table, and a chair converge, he can easily feel each object before moving toward it.

The blind child needs more practice at this skill than the sighted child, but the more he is allowed to cruise, the more confident he will become and the better prepared he will be for the next developmental step—independent walking.

When babies are cruising, they often are seen standing alone without support, trying to balance their bodies. This prerequisite for walking independently also occurs in the blind baby, but for him it is a more anxiety producing experience. When parents see their baby make his first attempts at standing alone, they should get close so that he can hear their familiar voices. To facilitate his taking a few steps independently, parents might place the baby about two inches in front of them, and call him and gently touch him, play a game of allowing him to move forward into their arms. This is a game many parents of sighted babies play. The baby can also be placed closely facing a wall and allowed to feel the distance between his body and the wall while the parent encourages him to move to the wall itself. These activities should be done in a playful manner and for short periods, so that they become a pleasurable experience for the child.

WALKING INDEPENDENTLY

While some blind babies begin to walk at the same age as sighted babies, around 12 to 16 months, many blind babies will take considerably longer before they finally let go. The blind baby may have all the skills of walking alone, yet holds on very lightly to a wall or a parent's hand out of fear. Some blind children don't let go until the age of two, and sometimes even a bit later.

When the baby begins walking alone, he has reached a phase in his development that places an additional burden on his parents. It is important that they realize why they must encourage the contact and exploration the child is now experiencing from an upright position.

Since the blind baby must rely on his memory of space and touch, not finding something in its expected place means it has disappeared entirely. As a result, it becomes difficult, if not entirely impossible, for the baby to form images and memories, possibly delaying his development in some ways. Parents have to assure continuity by seeing to it that furniture and other objects remain in the same places. The stability of the furnishings in the house becomes a point of reference to the baby's total orientation of himself and his relationship to the space around him.

During the time the blind baby is learning to walk, very few demands should be made on him and care should be taken not to provoke other anxieties and to shield him from them. Walking for a blind child requires much courage, and he needs a great deal of encouragement to try. To help him succeed, it may be advisable to make sure the soles of his shoes are of a rough texture to prevent slipping. If that is not possible, attaching strips of masking tape to the soles of his shoes sometimes helps. The rubber soles of sneakers, which grip the floor, can also give the baby the added security he needs. However, once the child has mastered walking, he will get better cues from leather soles, rather than rubber which eliminates sound and texture. As the blind child grows, he will learn to use those sounds and textures to orient himself. He will be able to judge the size of the room by the feedback he gets from the sound of his shoes. He can also feel different textures which give him additional information as to where he is.

If a blind child fails to learn to walk, intervention on the part of the parents may be needed. For instance, the baby may hold on to a stick with both hands while the mother gently pulls it toward her. If she lets go of her grasp of the stick, the baby may continue to walk toward her, as long as she keeps talking and touching him to assure him of her presence. A harness may also serve as a similar support, since the baby can feel the security of being held, yet at the same time has the freedom to move. Again, the mother may gradually let go of the harness until the baby learns to walk independently. For the blind child, the harness will have to be placed in reverse, with the lead in front, so that the mother can face the child and talk to him, her voice guiding him in the direction he is to move.

Many blind children walk stiff-legged, partly because of fear, partly because they cannot see others walk. A game most children, sighted or blind, enjoy, that may loosen the stiffness of a blind child, is to have the child walk with his feet on the parent's feet. It may also help to walk behind the child with the adult's knee bending the knee of the child as the child walks. This can be fun, and most children enjoy the exercise.

During the time the blind child is mastering the new skill of walking, he may, like the sighted child, become so fascinated with his own achievement that he refuses to stop, even when he is near exhaustion. He may not want to stop long enough to be fed or to go to bed, and should be treated the same as one would deal with any child going through the same stage.

Around the time the sighted child is learning to master gross motor skills of crawling, creeping, standing, cruising, and walking independently, he also experiments with climbing. Since the blind child is not attracted by the sight of steps, low stools, chairs, and sofas, he may have to be encouraged and given a little help by lifting his knee and giving him a boost. Although it is tempting not to teach a child to climb, the blind child should not be denied the enjoyment of learning this skill, which is the only way he can get a sense of height. Once any child has mastered climbing, he must learn where he must never climb.

Steps are a particularly great attraction to the sighted child. If the blind child is exposed to steps, he too will enjoy the challenge of climbing up and will do so without instruction. Coming back down, however, is difficult for all children. The blind child can learn to climb downstairs if he is shown how, by placing his feet on the step below. If possible, the parent should leave two or three steps free and block off the remainder; by placing a gate on the third step, the child can be allowed the freedom to learn with safety.

FINE MOTOR DEVELOPMENT

About the time sighted babies begin to walk, they are often seen practicing new skills of bringing thumb and forefinger together and picking up the minutest specks from the floor, table, or high chair tray. The blind baby will not be motivated to do so. This manual skill, which develops with experience, is important for all children since it helps them develop fine motor coordination and skills for such activities as placing small pegs, lacing, stringing beads, buttoning, and unbuttoning. The blind baby is not likely to develop these skills without adult intervention.

The simplest and most practical method of teaching a baby this skill is through the use of small bits of food. Cheerios, dry cereals, raisins, bits of cheese, etc., placed on a table or tray of the high chair serve as excellent motivators. These can be scattered about, two or three inches apart, and he can be shown where he can find them by placing his hand over each piece. At first the baby will have difficulty grasping the small pieces and will drop many of them, but occasionally he will get a piece into his mouth which will encourage him to try again. Since developing the skill requires much practice, snack time every day might be a good time for this exercise.

Chapter 3

SOCIAL DEVELOPMENT

FEEDING

The sighted infant usually gazes at the mother's face, feels her arms around him, feels the warmth and softness of her body, and hears her voice soothing him and talking to him while he is being fed. Since infants are usually awake during feeding time, they are more alert and attentive to sensation—sight, sound, touch, and smell. The blind baby, who cannot see his mother's face, has to depend on hearing, touch, and smell to experience the mother's closeness. Holding the baby while bottle-feeding him, and speaking softly to him, allowing as much body contact as possible, will increase his feeling of comfort and security and will lead to better awareness of his own body. Gently stroking the infant's body and placing his hands on the breast (if breast-fed) or the bottle will further enhance his feeling of closeness during feeding.

Early in his development, the sighted infant gradually learns to associate the distant visual image of the bottle with being fed. For the blind baby, sound has to replace the sight;

shaking the bottle so that it will produce a distinctive sound will alert the baby to the approaching bottle. Once he has learned to associate the sound of the bottle with actual feeding, he may open his mouth before the nipple reaches his lips. Signs of anticipation indicate that the baby has learned to sort out the various sounds around him and to make the correct association.

Babies eating strained food can be fed in several positions: sitting in the parent's arms, in an infant seat, or later in a high chair. Unless the blind baby is placed in a semi-upright position in the early months while being fed, he will get used to eating lying down. Once these habits are established, it may be difficult for the baby to make a change since he does not see other people sitting and eating.

Strained foods should be introduced as soon as the pediatrician recommends it. The blind baby needs a signal that food is approaching his mouth, for example, rattling the dish or the jar of food with the spoon before the spoon is put to his mouth. Before he is fed, the baby should be brought into the kitchen so he can hear other sounds associated with preparing his food, such as opening jars, heating food, or running the blender.

Unless care is taken to prepare the blind child for an imminent activity by using some auditory signal associated with that particular activity, the baby can easily be frightened, since he has no way of anticipating what is going to happen. The sighted child is always alerted by what he sees, and can prepare himself in advance. The blind child needs to be alerted through sound and touch. Once the child understands speech, an upcoming activity, such as a meal, can be verbalized.

Babies sometimes reject certain foods and they should not be forced to eat them. Instead, parents can reintroduce them at various intervals to see whether the baby will accept them.

After the baby has learned to eat strained foods, and if

the doctor consents, junior foods should be introduced. A delay in changing the consistencies of food may cause problems later on.

Once the baby begins to put his fingers and objects into his mouth, he can be given a teething biscuit. The introduction of a biscuit helps the baby learn the very first step of self-feeding, in addition to teaching him how to bite and exposing him to the texture of more solid food. The biscuits, which are hard, are both nutritious and tasty, do not crumble, and can be grasped and held easily. The baby can be shown how to hold a biscuit by placing his fingers around it and guiding his hand to his mouth. He may drop it several times, but with patience from the mother he will succeed.

Blind babies can learn to eat solid foods in much the same manner and at about the same time as sighted babies. Sighted babies sometimes indicate a desire to eat solid foods before a parent introduces them because they are attracted by what they see others eating and want the same. In this way, the sighted baby learns to enjoy a variety of table foods. Since the blind baby is unlikely to be attracted to food on the table he cannot see, it is up to the parent to offer the baby foods he might want if he could see them. Experiencing new foods stimulates the baby's palate; parents should make pleasurable sounds while presenting them.

Some babies have difficulty accepting solid foods and learning to chew. Parents often become upset or frightened when the baby gags when first presented with more solid food, and give up quickly. It would be wise for parents to reintroduce these foods at another time, perhaps at the beginning of a meal when the baby is most hungry. However, if the parent is having a difficult time feeding solid foods to the baby and the baby is merely swallowing foods without mashing them between his gums or gagging, we recommend that the parent begin very gradually, by introducing foods that easily melt in the mouth, such as vanilla wafers, graham crackers, and Cheerios. Small bits of these foods can be placed in the baby's mouth to give him the feeling of a more solid consistency without any fear of gagging. At other times, a parent can place half a teaspoon of peanut butter into the baby's mouth. Because peanut butter sticks to the roof of the mouth the baby is forced to move his tongue. Once the baby has learned to mash foods with his gums, bits of cheese, small cubes of bread, and small bits of fresh fruit can be placed one at a time between his gums on the side of his mouth.

Another method is to gradually add table food to the food the child will accept. For instance, if the infant will accept only soup or commercial baby food, mix one teaspoon of solid table food with the baby food at first and very slowly increase the amount until the child is eating more solid and firmer food. Some babies will eat a variety of foods but will accept them only if they are mashed or put through a blender. The principle illustrated in the previous example can be applied by gradually making the food coarser, in almost unnoticeable degrees. Parents can find their own creative methods of teaching the baby to eat solid foods when he is having a difficult time.

Feeding time for babies, whether sighted or blind, can be a time of closeness and of satisfaction, a time not only to still hunger, but to induce a feeling of intimacy and well-being. As the child develops, meals should be a time of togetherness and sharing of food, as well as of verbal exchanges of experiences with other members of the family. Although the blind child cannot see family members sitting around a table at dinnertime, he will still benefit from the experiences. The baby can hear others talking, discussing, and interacting while eating their dinner. The child's presence at the table is not enough however. Different family members need to speak to the child from time to time, to touch him, and to refer to something the child may be doing or eating.

Including the child at meals also allows the parents to expose the baby to the tastes, smells, and textures of the

different foods they are eating. The child can begin sitting
with the family during mealtimes as soon as he is old
enough to sit in the high chair. If he has already eaten, he
might be kept involved with a crust of bread or samples of
new foods.

Drinking from a Cup

A cup should be introduced to the baby as soon as he can
maintain a sitting position, although he may be unable to
hold the cup by himself or to control the flow of liquid into
his mouth. In order to prepare the child for future proper
eating habits, he should be started with a cup while sitting in
a high chair. This is often a messy procedure, especially for
the blind child, who will need more training in acceptable
eating habits. Since he is unable to imitate the behavior of
others, he must be shown in different ways.

Training cups, while commonly used with sighted
children, are not practical for the blind child because they
are deceptive: They have a plastic cover on top so the child
can move the cup in any way and nothing will spill. The cup
also hinders learning about cause-and-effect relationships.
The blind child will learn to drink from a regular cup,
although it may require more patience on the part of the
parents. However, they will be rewarded when they observe
the child's competence in handling a cup.

The child should explore the cup with both hands
before liquid is poured into it. It should also be introduced
when the child is thirsty. Using juice as the beginning liquid
is best, since the baby may associate milk with his bottle and
reject the cup for this reason. Once the child has learned to
drink from a cup, milk can be offered in it. If the baby then
rejects milk from a cup, allow about 20 minutes before
giving him a bottle, in order to avoid his associating
rejection of the cup with the reward of the bottle.

After the child has explored the cup and liquid has been
poured into it, the child's hands should be placed around it,

guided to his mouth, and helped to control the flow. He will need to be shown how to pick it up from the tray of the high chair and how to replace it. The baby has no difficulty picking up the cup from the tray, but replacing it takes him much longer than the sighted child. The more practice he gets, the sooner he will become competent at it. This skill is difficult for the blind baby because he not only has to learn to hold the cup in an upright position, but he must also judge the distance to the tray. In the early learning stages the blind child must use both hands in learning to control the cup; only later will he be able to control the entire action with one hand. If liquid is spilled, the child should be made aware of what has happened by bringing his hands into contact with the spilled liquid.

Many children, both sighted and blind, tend to throw the cup after they drink from it. The blind child may continue to do so for a longer period of time because he cannot see how others behave. As in many other areas, control, patience, and discipline need to be exercised.

FINGER-FEEDING

Learning to finger-feed is an important stage for the blind child, since it helps him make the association of how food gets from a plate, bowl, or dish into his mouth. In addition, it affords him the opportunity to feel the different textures of food. All children go through this stage of finger-feeding before using utensils to eat. It is an important, though very messy, phase. The blind child may take a bit longer passing through it because learning to handle a spoon efficiently is more difficult for him. Parents who find the mess disturbing can place newspapers or a plastic covering under the high chair. They may also wish to wear an apron and to move the high chair away from walls or furniture.

Except for dry snacks, which can be placed on the tray of the high chair, all food should be put on a plate, or in a bowl or dish. Since the child cannot see others eating, he will need to be shown that food is eaten from a plate. Just as with the cup, the child should be permitted to feel the entire plate, bowl, or dish with both hands before food is placed on it. When he is ready to eat, he will need to be shown where the food is by placing his hand on it, and then helped by guiding his hand to his mouth. The types of food used for finger-feeding are what all children eat with their fingers: fruit, meat, cheese, bread, cookies, vegetables, etc. Soups, ice cream, puddings, and the like should be fed with a spoon. However, the baby's hand must be placed on the spoon and, with the parent's hand over his, he must be made to feel how the spoon travels from the plate to the mouth. Some children throw their plate as well as their food. This, of course, needs to be discouraged. A firm tone, in addition to controlling the child's hands, may be necessary. If the child has difficulty accepting a plate, a rubber suction disk can be attached to the bottom of the plate and then suctioned to the tray of the high chair. This keeps the plate firmly attached to the tray and may help to control the child's impulse to throw his plate.

The child needs to be taught what to do with food he has tasted and rejected, because he cannot see how others dispose of it. A folded paper napkin in the corner of his tray makes an easily distinguishable area for discarded food. The parent's patience will be rewarded when it leads to the mastering of independent eating skills, and eliminates embarrassment when visiting or eating in a restaurant. Like any child, the blind baby should be expected to learn acceptable habits; he needs only to be shown.

SPOON FEEDING

After the blind child has mastered finger-feeding, he should be ready to use a spoon. Except for scooping, which takes him a little longer to learn, the child can soon use a spoon as skillfully as a sighted child. By this time, he should have become familiar with the feel of the spoon, having had his parent put his hand on it when feeding him foods that he could not pick up with his fingers. Now he has to learn to dip the spoon into the bowl, scoop the food, and bring it up to his mouth.

It is best to begin with foods the child particularly likes and that adhere to the spoon, such as puddings, ice cream, etc. Initially the food should be placed in a bowl rather than in a shallow plate, because scooping from a bowl is easier to learn. With the child's hand on the spoon and the parent's hand over his, the parent will direct his hand to the bowl, through a scooping movement, and then to his mouth. Since this takes the blind child longer to learn, the parent must be patient and persistent until the child has mastered it. While the child is learning to scoop food independently, he will probably be very messy at first and his movements uncoordinated. Much of the food may slide off his spoon and back into his bowl or onto his bib, and it will take quite a while before he can tell when his spoon is full and when he has lost the food. After he has learned to scoop fairly well, he should then be taught to hold the bowl with his other hand to keep it from slipping. If this is too difficult for the child, he can be helped by either using the suction disk or by the simpler method of keeping a wet napkin under his bowl to prevent it from sliding.

Like sighted children, blind infants develop many of their own individual styles of using a spoon. This may be permitted if it is efficient and socially acceptable. If the way in which a child uses a spoon will attract unnecessary attention to him, then it should be discouraged, and he should be taught to use the spoon in an appropriate manner. For the child who is unable to grasp a spoon for any reason, a spoon handle can be adapted to meet his needs. Some are commercially available.

First Steps in Dressing and Undressing

As soon as the blind baby can sit without support, his interest should be aroused in the activity of dressing and undressing. For instance, when the baby is being undressed his hand should be placed on his shoe and guided through the motion of taking it off. The same process can be repeated with the socks and other articles of clothing. In removing his shirt, it is best to pull it halfway over his head and with his hands on the shirt, gently pull it off. The same method applies to dressing, although this skill takes longer to learn. Making the child aware of dressing and undressing is necessary because he has no idea of the total action involved unless he experiences it himself. These activities should be done at appropriate times, such as when the baby is ready for a bath, sleep, or getting dressed to go outdoors.

The use of language is never to be forgotten in any of the activities suggested. When a parent goes through an action with the baby, or the baby comes into contact with an object, it must be named for him. For instance, if the mother is feeding the baby, the word "eat" must intermittently be used during feeding. When she undresses the infant, the word "shirt" needs to be said as she removes the shirt. When an object such as a spoon or a bell is placed in the child's hand, the object should be named. Using one word sentences when emphasizing the name of an object or activity is helpful at this time. Naming objects and verbalizing actions is important for all children. For the blind child it is particularly important because he cannot see objects or actions and has no way of remembering their names unless he is told.

Chapter 4

EMOTIONAL DEVELOPMENT

SEPARATION

At the time the baby, sighted or blind, begins to walk independently he generally begins to fear the very separation he seeks. The degree of anxiety the baby feels varies with the child and his experiences. It is not uncommon for the blind baby to constantly call out to his mother for reassurance of her presence. Understanding this, parents might help by keeping in touch with their child from time to time, talking to him, calling to him, or giving him an occasional hug.

Most babies at one time or another experience extended separation from their parents for one reason or another, such as the birth of a sibling, hospitalization, or an emergency trip. The separations are generally very difficult, especially during crucial stages of development. Separations can be more devastating for the blind baby because, unlike the sighted child who forms a visual image he can recall and hold onto, the blind baby has only the fleeting sensations of touch and sound. Therefore, whenever possible, adequate preparation for separations is suggested. The baby should meet the substitute caregiver several times before the parent's departure. The baby will need to feel the substitute's face and hair, hear her voice, and be held by her as much as possible beforehand, in order to become fully acquainted with her.

If possible, the substitute should come to the baby's home so the baby will remain in his own surroundings. Keeping the same routine and informing the substitute of the baby's habits may help the baby cope better during the parents' absence. This preparation is not unlike what one would do for a sighted baby, but is more important for the blind baby.

When the parents return, the baby's reaction will vary just as it does with sighted children. He may withdraw or become angry, fretful, or clingy. The parents should respond as they would to a sighted child, except the blind baby may need more reassurance through body closeness and voice. One might think that because the baby cannot see he will not be disturbed by separation, but this is not so.

SOCIAL DEVELOPMENT

There are infants, sighted or blind, who resist being held and who become stiff and irritable in their mothers' arms. For instance, babies who have spent time in an incubator often respond in this manner. If this is the case, it is important that the mother realize that she is not being rejected by the infant, but that her baby has not yet learned how to respond. Hold the infant for short periods at a time and increase the periods very gradually, and in time the baby will relax and eventually enjoy being held.

Blind babies are born with different temperaments and personalities and will react in different ways to sensory experiences, just as sighted babies do. Some infants like to be rocked, while others prefer to be held in certain ways. Some are more responsive than others. Some parents get discouraged if their child does not respond, and withdraw, which may further threaten the relationship, creating a vicious cycle.

Although the baby cannot see his parents, he can form the same attachments as the sighted child. In order to assure this, he will need closer and more frequent body contacts with them, more exposure to the touch of their hands, faces, and bodies as well as their voices. The baby needs the additional stimulation of being held, caressed, and spoken to. It is the only way he can get to know his parents; therefore, his waking hours should be a pleasurable experience that has meaning for him. Otherwise, he is vulnerable to living in a void. However, care must be taken that he is not overstimulated; too much stimulation can have the reverse effect, and the baby may withdraw.

The blind infant will respond to the mother's voice with a smile about the same time as the sighted infant. Eliciting this first smile is an important event for both baby and parents because it shows them that the baby is responding. This first smile can be crucial to the relationship between parent and baby, since the parents may still be recovering from the initial shock of their child's impairment and do not know what to expect. The smile not only reassures the parents of the normal feelings and reactions of their baby, but also gives the parents a feeling of being appreciated in turn by the child. One parent of a blind infant aptly stated, "When I saw him smile for the first time, my whole attitude and feelings changed. It made me feel I was doing something right." Inducing a smile from a baby comes naturally to most parents and they usually accomplish it by holding a baby close and talking to him in an endearing tone. For the blind baby, this experience is even more important since he cannot see his parents. Instead, he must "see" with his hands. Therefore, beginning at a very early age, his hands should be placed over his parents' faces while they talk to him.

For the first several months, most sighted babies are social creatures and smile readily at anyone who smiles at them. The blind baby will do the same except that he needs physical contact as well as to "hear" the smile in people's voices as they respond to his smile by touch or voice. As the sighted baby develops, he becomes selective, and begins to reserve his smiles for familiar faces. The blind baby will become equally discriminating, responding to some voices and not to others.

Many sighted babies often cling to their parents in a strange or new environment. Parents of blind babies are often surprised to find their blind baby react just as the sighted baby and knows when he is in an unfamiliar place. However, he may become more fearful than the sighted baby when he cannot interpret new sounds. To reassure him, he may need to be held closely. As he grows and understands speech the environment can be described to him. Until then, parents must be sensitive to their child's reactions to new situations.

In order to help the baby adapt to changes and to avoid fears later on, the parents need to expose the blind baby to experiences of daily living just as they would a sighted baby. Therefore, it is a good idea to take the baby out to various places; visiting friends and relatives, traveling on trains, buses, and cars; or going to stores.

Chapter 5

THE SENSES

Hearing

What we have said throughout is that the blind baby
learns and grows much as the sighted baby does, as long as
parents of blind babies understand how they learn and
provide the necessary intervention to facilitate the learning.

How do we stimulate and train a baby to use his other
senses optimally if he is born blind? From the very
beginning, especially throughout the child's early years,
parents of blind children need to constantly remember that
what he is missing visually the child must experience either
by sound, touch, smell, taste, or whatever minimal vision he
may have. This is often difficult for parents to keep in mind.
Educators, too, sometimes have to remind themselves to
instruct the blind child in some activities they assume the
child knows.

Hearing will become the most important link between
the blind child and the outside world. It is through hearing
that he will pick up the nuances in a voice that let him know
whether a person is smiling, angry, serious, or joking,

ich the sighted child sees by looking at the facial
ion. Later on, hearing will become a source of
ormation as the blind child judges distances—whether he
is far away from a wall, near a wall, headed toward traffic, or
walking away from traffic.

In order to develop the blind child's sensitivity and
ability to discriminate sounds, he needs to be taught to
listen. Teaching a child to listen begins in early infancy.
Since hearing is such a major source of information for the
blind child, caution must be taken in the development of its
use. Loud sounds, too much noise, and constant auditory
stimulation tend to dull the child's sensitivity and may
become a source of irritation, causing him to tune out. And
if the child tunes out sounds in his environment, he cuts off
this major contact with his world. Radios, television, and
record players must be used discriminately. In order for him
to be able to distinguish differences between various sounds,
the child must be exposed to them for short periods, and the
sounds he hears should be distinct and clear, and not
muffled or confused with background noises or music.

Parents of blind children are encouraged to talk to their
infants, but it is important that the parent's speech be clear.
At first, the child will perceive the tone of voice and begin to
interpret its meaning: soothing, reprimanding, angry. It
will take several months before he will start to attach
meaning to words. Since the blind baby cannot see what the
word refers to or to what the word belongs, it is important to
name for him what he can touch, hear, and smell; the objects
he holds and explores; parts of his body as he moves them or
as he is bathed or dressed; foods and utensils as he is fed; and
feelings as he cries or laughs.

Since he cannot see, he must be helped to localize sound.
This can be done by shaking a favorite toy in different
directions to the left or right of his body, in front and in back
of him, above his head, and so on. If he is unable to localize
the sound, the parent needs to help him by turning his head

in the appropriate direction. Before the baby is able to turn toward sound, the parent will know the baby is listening when he stops an activity. Only much later will he learn to reach for the object making the sound.

Musical toys such as a xylophone, toy piano, or small drum are good sources for learning to listen to sounds. Playing a high note and then a low note—giving the child contrasts in sounds—is a good beginning. If the mother is bringing a bottle to the baby from another room, she might begin talking to him before she arrives, so the baby can hear her approach by the increasing loudness of her voice.

When selecting sound-making toys, it is wise to select contrasting sounds rather than ones that are similar so that the child learns more easily to differentiate between the toys. Parents can also use homemade toys by placing a noise-making object such as a bell, rice, water, or a key inside a small plastic bottle. Caution must be taken that the bottle is sealed tightly and that the objects used are large enough not to be swallowed.

When the child is crawling or walking, the parent can begin to play games in which the baby needs to not only localize a sound but move toward it, for example having him follow the flush of a toilet or listen to running water in the sink, a record player, television, the sound of a blender, or vacuum cleaner. If the child is unable to do so at first, taking his hand and going along with him may be necessary. It is helpful to play these games when there are no other sounds to distract him.

Eye contact is a very important factor in getting a sighted infant's attention. While the blind baby misses this contact, his parents miss it even more and often feel "cheated" and "let down" when their baby fails to return their glance. The parents of the blind baby must call his name and also make physical contact with him in order for the child to learn to attend when his name is called, and must always remember to call the baby's name before beginning to speak so the child becomes aware that what is said is meant for him; otherwise, he has no way of knowing for whom it was intended. Moreover, everbody entering the room where a blind child is should make his presence known and identify himself.

Sounds that are heard in the environment should be named for the baby once he has learned to sit independently. However, as soon as the baby has begun to understand a few words, labelling sounds is insufficient, because, although he can learn to say "bell" when he hears a bell, he will have no idea what a bell is unless he comes into contact with it and learns its function. Therefore, when the doorbell rings the child should be taken to the doorbell, he should feel it, and ring the bell himself. Only in that way will he know what a doorbell is and its function. This kind of learning should be afforded for most sounds the child hears, such as running water, egg beaters, blenders, vacuum cleaners, and electric shavers.

TOUCH

From the moment parents know their child is blind, they need to remember that their baby will "see" the world mainly with his hands. Therefore, it is important for the blind baby to learn from the very start that information comes through his hands. Although a very young infant may not be aware of and may not know what he is touching, it is necessary for the blind baby to experience touching and feeling whenever possible. The sighted young infant who searches with his eyes cannot always interpret what he sees, but we can assume that some information is reaching him. The blind baby needs the same stimulation, except that it has to come through his hands instead. Some blind children have difficulty accepting the feel of certain textures, and since the blind baby's hands are of such great importance to him, the earlier parents begin introducing surfaces and textures of all kinds to him, the more accepting he is likely to be when it will serve more important purposes later on.

As was suggested previously, the baby's hands should be placed on the breast or bottle while being fed. When the mother talks to the infant, she should place his hands on her face and mouth. When the infant is being prepared for his bath, changed, or dressed, his hands should be guided to touch his skin including his head, face, and feet. While he is still naked, a variety of soft textures might be used to stroke parts of his body, such as pieces of fur, satin, soft cotton, terry cloth, or wool. These fabrics should also be placed in his hands to feel, and under his soles as well, helping him to become aware of differences in textures and providing him with sensory stimulation. If the baby withdraws, his feet should be stimulated first, and gradually his legs, then his body and face.

When the baby is able to sit in the high chair, many objects of various shapes should be placed in his hands. Parents should remember that the sighted baby not only reaches and touches objects earlier than the blind baby does, but he explores visually many, many objects and people in his environment. The blind baby should not be deprived; parents must be conscious of the fact that if the baby does not come into contact with objects in his environment, then as far as he is concerned they do not exist.

When an object is placed in the baby's hands, he needs to be shown how to explore it with his palms and fingertips, running both his hands over the entire object to experience texture, size, shape, and temperature. The object should be named, using only one word, such as "cup," "spoon," "soap," or "ball." When the child has learned how to feel objects, give him time to explore them, since exploring with one's hands is more time consuming than observing with one's eyes. If the baby puts the object to his forehead, cheek, or mouth, allow him to do so: He may be trying to "see" better. Once he learns to use his hands more effectively, he will no longer need to use other parts of his body. He also needs to be introduced to a variety of objects frequently, so he will begin to realize that there are differences in sizes, shapes, textures, and temperatures. Later on, he will be able to identify them and name them. Parents often limit the objects their blind baby touches to toys. Common everday objects, such as measuring cups, measuring spoons, wooden spoons, plastic jars, keys, sponges, small boxes, wooden bowls, and numerous other household articles that can be safely handled, should be explored. The sighted baby sees all these objects; parents of blind babies need to make an effort to have their baby "see" them with his hands. A six-month-old sighted baby in his parent's arms or in a walker will generally try to touch everything within sight and reach because he is visually attracted to objects and becomes curious.

When a child begins to crawl, creep, cruise, or walk, he should be allowed to explore and touch as much as possible of the environment with which he comes in contact. The same precautions employed for the safety of sighted children should be used with the blind child, and objects precious to the adult should be removed as they would be from around the sighted child. Some parents prefer to leave certain objects exposed; in that case, the same disciplinary actions used for sighted babies can be used to remind the blind baby not to touch them.

Parents have told us that they have not permitted their sighted children to take out and handle the items in the kitchen cabinet that were safe for handling but have done so for their blind children, since they wanted to encourage their curiosity and teach them about their environment. The sighted baby has the opportunity of seeing what is inside a kitchen cabinet, whereas the blind baby only knows what is inside by exploring it tactually. It is at this point, when the child is beginning to move about, that it is most important to name objects he comes in contact with. This is important for all babies, but more so for the blind baby because it affords him the opportunity of later relating the name of the object to the tactile experience he has had. A sighted baby has constant reinforcement by seeing; the blind baby needs to rely on previous tactile experiences, the only experience he has to relate to.

Outdoor experiences are equally important for the blind child while he is still an infant in the carriage. In no way will he know what rain, snow, or wind are unless he feels them. One two year old who had never been taken to the park cried bitterly every time the wind hit his face because he had never been exposed to it before. The earlier a parent begins offering his child all kinds of experiences, the easier learning becomes.

SMELL

Smell is the least appreciated of all our senses; if they had to give up one of their senses, most people would probably select the sense of smell. However, we have made it a point to train the parents of blind children to stimulate this sense as early as possible. Sharpening this sense and making the most use of it will help the child integrate smells with other information he receives through his ears and hands and whatever minimal vision he may have. Therefore, as soon as the baby is able to sit independently, parents should begin to expose the baby to different scents that occur in daily living. When parents are preparing food, opening up a can of coffee or peanuts, a box of cake, or a jar of baby food, they should encourage the baby to smell it by holding it close to his face. When the baby is in the bathroom, have him smell the soap, baby powder, baby oil, or any other product you may be using. Many of the scents the baby will pick up anyway but it is wise to make the baby aware that his nose can tell him what is around. This kind of stimulation will help him develop and sharpen his perceptiveness.

As the baby gets a little older and begins to understand words, name the scents. Before he eats, encourage him to smell his food so he learns to distinguish differences by scents as well as by touch. When daddy is shaving or brushing his teeth, have the baby smell the shaving cream and toothpaste. If a sibling gets new shoes or mother uses perfume, involve the baby by having him smell it. As he grows and learns, he will recognize from a distance many things, including foods, by their smell.

SLEEP

Disturbances of sleep that may arise, such as difficulty in putting the blind baby to sleep, frequent awakening during the night, or very early awakening, are also observed by parents of sighted babies. The earlier a routine of normal sleep patterns is established and maintained, the better for the baby and his family. Most parents are aware of the importance of a quiet period prior to bedtime. Giving the baby a little more attention and affection during this time, and not rushing, can be pleasant for both the baby and the parents.

When the blind baby is old enough to understand a few words, sitting with him before bedtime with a basket of simple everyday objects, such as a set of keys, a plastic cup, a spoon, a comb, or a plastic dish, and naming the objects for him while he feels them, one at a time, can be the equivalent to looking at baby's first picture book. If the infant is too restless for this type of activity, perhaps he needs to be rocked and sung to before bedtime. Knowing one's baby and what relaxes him is important.

Many parents of blind babies who have sleep disturbances attribute them to the child's inability to distinguish daylight from darkness. True, blind babies cannot make that distinction, but they can hear the difference in the level of noise and activity. Some blind babies may confuse day and night, but so do some sighted babies. In cases in which the child reverses sleep habits and continues to do so over a long period, other causes should be looked into; blindness is not the reason.

Chapter 6

PLAY

PLAY

We often hear parents say "he is only playing" or "this is child's play," expressions conveying the impression that play has little or no value, that it is easy and a waste of time. The opposite is true. Play for the growing child is serious work. It is through play that the child learns about his environment. Play is the laboratory in which the child experiments to discover how things work, including his own body; how far he can reach and how high; the puzzle of the smaller fitting into the bigger; the disappearance of objects and how to find them; softness, hardness, smoothness, and roughness; the round and the square—all discovered through endless repetitions and trial and error. For the sighted child, these discoveries are made easier by looking and watching. The blind child has only touch and sound to guide and teach him. He must therefore be given every opportunity to experiment with toys, with things in the house, so that in his own way he may make the same discoveries and experience the same satisfaction from his rewarded curiosity.

Since the child will not be attracted to objects and toys by sight, he must be brought into contact (touch) with them. Without intervention, the blind child will not learn to play. His hands will have to be guided during the first encounters before he can take over. Once he knows an object, he will explore further and invent his own "play" with it. It has been a source of continuous fascination for us to observe young blind children understanding without difficulty and without being taught that the small toy objects represent the larger "real" articles. They use them in make-believe activities, pretending to drink from an empty cup, feeding the toy doggie or doll, etc. Understanding the transposition of sizes seems to be an innate gift the blind child shares with his sighted counterpart.

Play begins in early infancy. Sighted babies who lie in their cribs and in their playpens spend much of their time looking and watching, gradually perceiving and discovering visual images and recognizing outlines, shapes, sizes, and colors. The blind baby cannot do this. Here again, intervention is necessary: The blind infant must be given the opportunity for discovery. More than the sighted baby he needs the stimulation of touch and sounds, which can easily be provided by attaching sound to otherwise silent objects. Mobiles are a good starting point. The mobiles for the blind baby can be made out of plastic disks, beads, keys, balls, or small balloons with bells inside. These objects can be strung across the crib or playpen, close to his body but slightly to the sides, so that when his hands flail about, he accidentally comes in contact with an object. Four objects should be sufficient, two on each side. Later on, to help the baby bring hands to midline, these objects can be placed in the center as well. The objects are leading to the child's beginning awareness of the world outside his own body, and the arousal of his curiosity about it.

In designing a tactile and auditory mobile for the baby care should be taken to secure the mobile firmly so that when the child grasps an object, holds on to it, or hits it, he does not get tangled in the string or elastic or pull it off. Of course, objects must not have sharp edges or be harmful in any way. Mobiles should not be used for more than one-half hour, two or three times a day, so the baby will not become bored with them. If the mobiles are changed, he can experience a greater variety of stimuli, and will be exposed to an element of surprise. Mobiles can also be used, adjusted to various heights, when the baby is sitting. They can be changed and rotated periodically, and new objects added from time to time.

There are several mobiles on the market that are appropriate for the blind child because they create sound when they are hit or have differing textures. Some parents have preferred to improvise on these by adding other objects to them.

Another method of paralleling the activity of the sighted baby, who observes his hands when they are moving about and becomes aware that he can control these movements, is to tie a soft string to the blind baby's wrist and connect it to the mobile. In that way he can begin to make the association between hand movements and the sound that is produced when he moves his hand.

Just as it is important to provide the baby with some kind of auditory stimulation as he uses his arms, it is important to stimulate the movements of his legs he cannot see. Instead of attaching the string to the baby's wrist and to the mobile, the string can be attached to the baby's ankle and mobile. The string should not be attached to both the leg and arm at the same time, so the baby can clearly differentiate whether he is moving his arm or his foot. Needless to say, supervision during these activities is of utmost importance, so the baby does not get tangled in the string.

Mobiles set up to be hit by the baby's hands should also be placed where he can accidentally hit them with his feet. Some commercially made mobiles do provide devices the baby can kick with his feet. Other possibilities are large inflatable toys that produce a squeaking noise when they are slightly squeezed. These very large toys can be placed at the baby's feet, so that when he kicks he can hear the sound that they produce and he can also feel the textures of these toys.

As the amount of time the baby spends awake increases, the mother should move the baby about with her as she works in different rooms of the house or apartment. The baby may be placed in an infant seat, a small cardboard box, or a playpen, or on a rug near the mother. The baby can then hear the mother as she moves about and talks or sings to him and is aware that she is nearby and he is not in a vacuum without sight or sound or any external stimulation. Objects can be placed in his hand, since one must always remember that the blind baby who does not come tactually in contact with objects or who does not hear them has no way of knowing where they are or, in fact, where he himself is and what is going on around him. Moving the child from one place to another during the day also increases the baby's awareness, his curiosity, and his ability to adapt to changes.

There will be times during the day when the parent is unable to spend time with the baby. During this time, a radio, record player, or music box might be turned on so the baby is auditorily stimulated while his parent is busy. However, as explained previously, such equipment should not be used continuously, nor simultaneously with other sounds or voices in the immediate environment.

Many parents ask about special toys for the blind baby. Most toys on the market that are used for sighted babies can be used and enjoyed by the blind baby as well. Often, household objects such as plastic bowls, plastic bottles, small boxes, plastic cups, old keys strung together, various papers that produce a sound, empty spools tied together, and pie plates are as effective and enjoyable as any expensive toy. Rattles can be made from small plastic bottles filled with beads, popping corn, or rice. Of course, the parent should be careful that the lids are tightly secured. As the baby gains better control of his hands, "busy boxes" can be tied to his crib or playpen and he can play with devices in which a string is pulled to produce a sound. Clutch balls, balls with bells inside, squeak toys, bracelets on a chain, bells on a chain, and stuffed animals can all be enjoyed by the baby when he is in the crib or playpen. These objects must be placed within his reach, a few at a time. If he loses a toy, he needs to be shown how to search for it by moving his arm around his body in a sweeping gesture.

If the parents suspect their baby has some vision, attaching a mirror to the crib or playpen so he can see some reflection of himself, even if it is just a shadow or movement of his body, is helpful. Even if the baby is unable to see an image of his body, he may at least get some visual stimulation through the changing light reflections in the mirror.

As early as two months, both sighted and blind babies begin to vocalize. When they do produce sounds, most parents are so delighted they automatically respond by "talking" back to the baby. In a very short time, vocal communication is established between the parents and the baby.

Any activity that offers the child closer contact with his parents through body touching and movement, through voice, and through smell, not only will help him to know his parents, but will increase his awareness of his own body and its movements. Holding the baby on one's lap, guiding his hands to touch one's body, making sounds and noises that will amuse him, and giving back to him whatever sounds he produces will soon elicit smiles and vocalization from the blind baby, just as they do in the sighted infant. Changing the volume of the voice from soft to loud, from high to low pitches, and repeating utterances of sounds stimulate the child's own sound production.

Games such as Ride a Cock Horse, which involves crossing the knees over and placing the baby on the free foot while holding his hands, and raising and lowering the foot rhythmically, are enjoyed equally by all infants. Riding piggy-back on daddy's shoulders while he is creeping on the floor is much fun for the child, and will give the baby a feeling of movement in the space he cannot see. Interestingly enough, blind babies enjoy Peek-a-Boo as much as their sighted contemporaries, when the necessary adjustments are made for their lack of vision. It may be played by placing a soft hat over the parent's head and letting the child pull it off to find and feel the parent's face. The game can be reversed by putting the hat over the baby's head. As in all situations, unfamiliar objects should be introduced by letting the child touch, move, and try them out to get to know them.

A little later, touching parts of his body and naming them can be made into the universal mother-child game of "touch your nose," "where are my ears?" etc. The young blind child will need a little more help than the sighted baby, since he cannot see the mother's face and has to be allowed to thoroughly explore it after having touched parts of his own face, and later parts of his own body. (The sighted child does not see his own face either, until he is old enough to understand his mirror image.)

As the baby grows and learns to walk, the sighted infant gets into and touches everything in sight. He learns how to open cupboards, push doors open, climb on chairs, and turn light switches, turn knobs on radios and TV sets, etc. Some blind babies can be just as mischievous, finding their way around the house or apartment and getting into as many things as their sighted peers do. But the majority of blind babies will not open cabinets, climb, etc., unless they are shown how (Figure 6-1). It is tempting not to show the blind baby how to turn knobs on radios and how to climb, but unless they practice all these skills they will not keep up with the development of sighted babies. A great deal of learning goes into playing with pots and pans that fit into each other, covers that fit, small boxes that can be stacked, spoons that

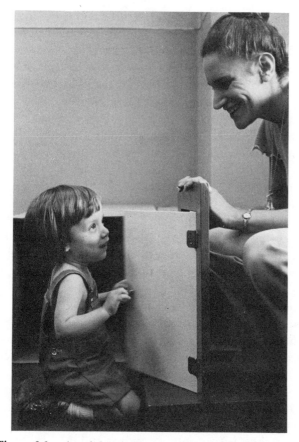

Figure 6-1. An eighteen-month-old boy learning to open and close a door.

can be dropped into a pan, and so on. We suggest that parents arrange one low cabinet in the kitchen to contain objects safe to handle that the baby can play with, and that they show the baby how he can stack small cans, drop spoons into pans, or put pots inside each other. Many of these concepts are difficult for the blind baby to learn, but he must not be denied the experience.

Our experience in working with blind children has

shown us that there is a gap in the development of blind children between the age they begin to walk and the time of their language acquisition. During this period, sighted children tend to become very interested in toys that have graduated sizes, such as stacking rings, cups, building towers, barrels that fit into each other, pegs that fit into holes, formboards, and formboxes. We have found that the blind child does not seem to be interested in such activities during this period, but catches up and learns to utilize this equipment and enjoy it when he is a bit older. The sighted child usually acquires the skills necessary to manipulate these toys visually. We assume the blind child needs another level of conceptual development which he does not reach until he is older. His tactile sense does not seem to be as reliable a source of concept formation and memory as is vision. Nor has his language development progressed sufficiently at this stage to help him comprehend verbal directions or to solve problems. During this time, the blind baby seems to predominately enjoy sound-making infant toys, lap games with his parents, and just handling objects.

However, here too, intervention is suggested. The child should be encouraged to use such toys for brief periods so he can become familiar with them and so the parents can become more aware at what point the child does become interested and able to acquire the skills necessary for their use (Figure 6-2). Parents should, however, be careful not to frustrate the child and not to become anxious. They must remember that this lag usually disappears as soon as the child acquires more experience, skill, and language. To help the blind child discriminate sizes he cannot see, parents might begin by first introducing very large and very small— but otherwise identical—objects, one fitting into the other, and let the child play with them before he is expected to place a variety of slightly graded objects one into the other. For this purpose various toys on the market can be used, such as graded cups, barrels that fit into each other, and a spindle

Figure 6-2.   A twenty-month-old girl using an educational toy.

with graded rings on it. These toys should be presented to the child on a tray so that he does not become preoccupied with searching for those that roll away or fall off.

We mentioned that at this stage children like to open doors. We feel opening and closing doors deserves a special paragraph because of its importance. Opening and shutting doors can be a dangerous activity for a sighted child, but even more so for the blind child, who cannot see the distance between the opening and the closing area and might hurt himself or other people. However, the blind child should be permitted to open and shut a door under the parent's supervision. Blind children eventually learn how to be careful with doors, and they have no more accidents than their sighted peers. However doors that are left ajar can be a real hazard. Some serious accidents have occurred when blind adults have smashed into a door that was left *half* open. It would be wise for family members to remember to shut a door completely or leave it open completely, but never to leave it half way.

Many toys on the market appear to be inappropriate for a sighted child, let alone for a blind child. Very few toys are designed specifically for blind children. Our experience has shown that many of the commercially produced toys suitable for a sighted child can be utilized by the blind child or can be adapted for his use. There is value to a blind child's ability to use toys made for a sighted child, since it enables him to feel that he has something in common with either his sighted peers or his sighted siblings and does not make him feel different.

Many manufacturers indicate the age for which a toy is appropriate. We have found that these age indications are very often grossly inaccurate. These age specifications should be disregarded; instead, toys should be purchased that will interest the child and challenge his curiosity, yet that he can learn to master easily.

Often toys bought commercially are not what they appear to be on the package or illustration; therefore, the parent should try to use the toy before it is purchased or presented to the child. This suggestion is valid for parents of sighted as well as blind children. The parent of a blind child may want to blindfold himself when he tries out the toy to better understand some of the difficulties that the child may encounter. This will not only enhance the parent's understanding of what the child needs in order to use the toy, but will also help the parent develop skills and new techniques to introduce the toy to the child. Each time a parent blindfolds himself, he may become aware of new facets of the skills required of the blind child to master the activity. However, when parents blindfold themselves, their perception of an object will be quite different from that of the congenitally blind child; the interpretation the parent makes when he feels an object is based on his having seen it visually.

If the parent finds it difficult to recognize an object tactually the blind child will find it doubly difficult.

Parents and other adults introducing a blind child to new toys should remember that the child needs to be shown at the beginning how a toy can be used. When a sighted child is introduced to a new toy, he has the opportunity to observe its use, size, color, shape, and function for as long as he wishes before he engages in play on his own. Since the blind child cannot see a toy or watch its use, he should be allowed to feel and explore it until he feels comfortable with it. He may need a little time to familiarize himself with it before he can enjoy it.

Although toys can be used in many ways and on many different levels, the child also needs to be taught to use toys properly and in their intended way, lessons the sighted child often acquires at a glance. If the blind child is consistently using a toy the same way for long periods, he should be distracted or the toy should be replaced with another one. The use of a toy in an all too repetitive manner does not necessarily indicate a child is enjoying the toy or that it is too easy for the child. It may be an indication that the child is losing himself in the activity and has difficulty stopping. On the other hand, if you find your child is experimenting or imaginatively using toys, he should be encouraged as long as his interest lasts.

The sighted child is usually interested in looking at very simple picture books and pointing to objects depicted when they are named by the parent and then later naming the pictures on his own. For the blind child, a similar activity can be introduced using a three-dimensional object instead of a two-dimensional picture. For the blind child, the previously mentioned object basket should be provided. At the beginning, these objects should be those that the child is fairly familiar with from his day-to-day activities. A parent can sit down with the child and name the object as he handles it. A few weeks later, the child can be asked to hand the parent a particular object that the parent has named. Only later will the child be able to name the object himself. The use of this basket of objects should be similar to the use of a simple picture book that parents often use with their sighted children. At times, objects which are miniatures of larger items can be used; however, they should be truly like the real objects in look and feel, although they may be reduced in size. The objects should be changed as the child grows and acquires more words.

Chapter 7

BLINDISMS AND MANNERISMS

Blindisms are best described as mannerisms that are peculiar to blind children. Some of the mannerisms blind children frequently develop are rolling the head, letting the head droop, rocking, jumping up and down, flapping the hands, and pressing the fingers against the eye or eyes.

Many blindisms begin very early in infancy. We have seen fingers pressed against the eyes as early as five months of age. Once a blindism becomes established, it is very difficult to get rid of, and parents often worry about such mannerisms' social acceptability. Even after the blind child is older and able to exercise some control, he is often seen regressing —using blindisms—when he is tense, anxious or excited. Stimulating the child or engaging him in activities seems to reduce and sometimes stops these symptoms.

The blind child who walks with his head drooping can be helped by simply lifting his chin. As he gets older, he can be reminded to keep his head up, and in addition, can be taught to turn toward the person speaking to him.

Rocking is one of the most common blindisms, and can begin in the crib. We suggest that parents put their hand on the child's shoulder to halt his rocking and at the same time distract him. When the child is older, he can be reminded that rocking is distracting to others and that other children do not do it.

Head rolling can also be diminished by simply placing a hand on the child's head and distracting him with an activity. He can be taught to control this blindism as he gets older.

Fingers pressed against the eye or eyes is the blindism that is the least understood. Some children rest the knuckle of their index finger against one eye; some use two fingers and some use both hands and rest both knuckles against both eyes. It would almost appear as though they are aware of their sensory loss.

Punitive action or nagging only serves to build more tension, which may increase the blindisms. A quiet hand on the child and distracting him generally are effective when the child is still young. When he is older, he can be reminded that his behavior is not socially acceptable. If he is motivated to behave like his peers blindisms generally diminish or disappear, though they may recur under stress.

Part II
THE TODDLER:
FROM TWENTY-THREE MONTHS
TO THREE YEARS

Chapter 8

THE BODY

Mobility

The toddler stage is a developmental milestone of immense significance for any child, sighted or blind. Once the child can walk independently, he perceives his world from a different angle. He has a powerful drive to master gross motor skills at this stage and to satisfy his growing curiosity about his environment. A sighted toddler is in almost constant motion, full of energy. He goes nonstop, pushing, pulling, climbing, touching, opening and closing doors, turning knobs, turning switches, carrying objects, dropping them, picking them up. He's also fascinated by small bits of paper he sees on the floor and tries to pick them up. He loves to test his body in space and will try to fit into drawers and to crawl into closets, cabinets, or any small enclosure he sees. When taken outdoors, he can hardly be contained; he will run and test his newly found power, attracted to what he sees, sometimes getting into dangerous situations. For the sighted child, the world is full of wonderful things to see, to touch, to feel, and to explore.

However, his wonderful world is also fragmented and still disorganized. He does not completely comprehend cause-and-effect relationships; for example, he does not understand that if he pulls a wire connected to a lamp, it will topple over. However, through vision and experience, the parts will soon fall into place, and the sighted child acquires more understanding of what he sees and experiences.

What happens to the blind toddler? The average blind toddler is likely to be far less active than the sighted toddler because he lacks the visual stimuli that propel his sighted peer. If the blind toddler shows little or no interest in moving about and exploring his environment, his parents may need to help arouse his curiosity and to show him all the exciting challenges that surround him. They may wish to examine what sparks the sighted toddler's curiosity and expose the blind child to the same experiences. Parents of blind children must not forget that although some sighted toddlers are not as curious or active as others, they do learn by merely looking. The blind toddler, however, has to be brought into contact with the objects in his environment. If he does not appear to enjoy some of the activities sighted toddlers do, he may need more time, and perhaps a more gradual introduction to new experiences. For example, the mother can put the child's hands on hers while she explores an object, and then gradually remove hers. In introducing the child to the sandbox, for example, the parent can step inside the sandbox with the child and hold him while he feels the sand, first gradually, pouring some on his arm or leg, and later into his hands. Since he cannot see the entire sandbox, nor other children playing in it, he may be frightened. Some very cautious sighted toddlers sometimes need these same slow introductions to new experiences.

The blind child has the added disadvantage of not perceiving objects in their entirety. Therefore, without intervention, the fragmentation of objects will continue for the child. For example, when he pulls open the door of a kitchen cabinet, the only area with which he comes into contact is the area his hand touches. Unless the parent makes sure he feels the entire cabinet, the child will not know the other parts exist. To familiarize the child with the cabinet, the parent must guide his hands along its surface, top, and sides so that the child will feel and perceive size and depth. In this way, he can be made to touch the shelves and objects on them. Similarly, the movement of doors opening and closing —the delight of all toddlers—can be introduced. To allow the toddler to develop a sense of depth, empty shelf or cabinet space should be made available to him for crawling inside. This will also give him the feeling of discovery and provide an impetus for further exploration. Once again, his hands must be guided to touch the entire area. If appropriate furniture is not available or the parent is uncomfortable with this kind of activity, similar experiences can be provided by making available to the child empty cardboard boxes into which the child can crawl.

Once the blind toddler is able to walk, he needs to be given reason to walk. The sighted toddler is constantly motivated to move because he is visually attracted to the many things around him and wants to reach them. The blind toddler must be motivated. He can be enticed to move around the house, for example, to fetch his toys and put them away. These little errands serve several purposes: They provide him with the opportunity to orient himself in the home and to learn where things are kept, and they also lead to more independence. Furthermore, they enhance and reinforce language by the use of words referring to position in space, such as in, on, on top, under, behind, and in front of. At first, the parents will have to go along with the child until he remembers where things are kept.

Blind children will usually not walk freely unless they are extremely familiar with an environment. Just as the blind baby learned to move freely in his crib or playpen as soon as he was familiar with it, so will the blind toddler move in space once he has learned its boundaries. Parents should not expect their toddler to walk freely in an unfamiliar environment. Instead, they should tell the child where he is and what it looks like before taking his hand and leading him around the room to explore it. Some blind toddlers, when they do walk independently, automatically protect themselves from bumping into objects by walking with their arms extended forward. However, the majority of blind children do not walk in such a manner. Most of them walk with a hesitant and cautious step, without using their arms to protect themselves; although they may bump into things occasionally, they are rarely seriously hurt because they generally move slowly. Overreacting to a bump or a fall may induce the blind child also to overreact. Parents should respond the same way they would do for any child. However, there may be times a blind child will have to be cautioned that an obstacle in his path, such as the sharp edge of a table, may hurt him if he is not careful. In such instances, describing what is ahead of the blind child will prevent trouble; for example, "Jimmy, there is a table in front of you," or "Johnny, there is a box near your foot. Don't trip on it." Merely telling the child to be careful gives him little information except to caution him; it is more helpful to tell him where and what the obstacle is. A few blind children are not cautious and constantly bump into things. These children will have to be shown how to extend their arms forward to protect themselves. If a parent feels his toddler can follow such directions, he should tell him the proper, most efficient position: to place his arm (left or right—whichever is easier), bent at the elbow, in front of him without touching his body, thus shielding the upper part of his torso.

When a blind child begins to walk, a whole new world opens up for him, a world he will be more eager to explore if it is interesting. The toddler stage is a difficult time for most parents, whether their child is blind or sighted. During this phase all children need to be carefully watched and supervised, and it is a good idea to remove all objects and articles that might be dangerous. Parents should allow the blind toddler as much time as possible to stop and explore as he walks around in order to allow him to develop and satisfy his curiosity. But most of all, he needs to learn that his environment can be interesting—and he will not know what is there unless he touches it, hears it, or smells it.

To help the toddler learn about his environment we encourage all parents to introduce the trailing method of mobility. Trailing is the hand contact a child maintains with walls or furniture while walking in a room or hall: the back of the hand, held at waist level, maintains gentle contact with the walls or furniture. Trailing allows the child more independence and teaches him the shape and dimensions of a room. He will gradually build a mental image of the room, remembering the arrangement of the furniture, objects, and appliances as points of reference to orient himself. For example, if he temporarily loses his way, he will remember that the refrigerator is next to the sink or that the couch is next to the table. The majority of blind toddlers have no difficulty finding their way around their homes.

Trailing will remain a way for the blind child to see an entire room. To facilitate the child's memory of shape and dimension, language should accompany his excursions into the environment, and it is important to name whatever he touches. Moreover, when possible, the child should be encouraged and helped to feel as much of an object as possible. For instance, the child's hands might be placed, palms down, on the surface of the table top to allow him in sweeping motion to experience the entire surface. Then his hands should be guided along the edges to give him a sense of shape. At this time, the toddler may not understand exactly what it is he is touching. It must be emphasized that in order for the blind toddler to become familiar with his environment and move a bit faster, it is important to keep furniture in the same place to facilitate memory and recall. Items such as toys and clothing should always be put in the same place so the child can locate them and return them. Once he can remember an object, it will serve as a point to orient himself.

BODY CONCEPT

The sighted toddler has seen most of his body as he moves parts of it or as they are being moved for changing, dressing, and playing. He has also seen his face and body in mirrors and taken delight in finding his image: "It's me!" Moreover, almost from the time he was born, he has been looking at other people's faces and bodies as they move about, especially his mother's. Later on, he has looked at pictures of people in different positions and activities. None of this has been available to the blind toddler. Yet he, too, will have to develop a sense of "me," an awareness of his body, his place in space, and his body's range of movements —the basis for his body concept, which will expand to include his feelings about himself and will influence his relationships with others.

The toddler, like the infant, should be helped and encouraged to move and touch parts of his body as well as to explore the parent's body. He should know by name and be able to point on verbal request not only to parts of his face, but to parts of his body as well—arms, legs, shoulders, elbows, knees, toes, etc. He might be given toy animals or dolls and asked to identify their body parts. If he has siblings, body contact should be encouraged.

RUNNING

Most blind children have difficulty running because they do not see others do it; they cannot imitate them.

Figure 8-1. Learning to run.

Moreover, they do not know their environment and its boundaries well enough to feel secure running in it. During the toddler stage, parents can take the child's hands and run with the child (Figure 8-1). Blind toddlers generally love this fast movement although they have difficulty accomplishing it by themselves.

SWIMMING

We suggest that parents introduce the blind child to a pool when he is very young, not necessarily to learn how to swim, but simply to enjoy the water. When the child is ready to actually swim, he will be well acquainted with water; this will make learning how to swim much easier for him. This is of special importance to the blind child because being immersed in water creates a new sensation for his entire body.

Many blind children whose feet cannot touch the bottom of the pool are sometimes frightened because they have no idea of the water's depth. Some sighted children may also be frightened, but they, at least, can see people standing. We found that as soon as the blind child was tall enough to keep his chin above water when his feet barely touched the bottom, his fear was quickly eliminated. We also found that it sometimes helped to give the child a stick long enough for him to feel the bottom so he knew the pool had a bottom to it.

An excessive amount of fear will have to be treated slowly, and the blind child, like a sighted one, must be reassured. It is helpful in such instances to have the child begin by playing outdoors in a small basin of water. He can then be introduced to a portable outdoor pool. If he is still frightened, he should not be expected to get into the pool right away. He can be encouraged to play with the water while sitting on the outside of the pool. This generally helps the frightened child.

Once the child has learned to feel comfortable in a pool, it is interesting to see him walk in the water at the same rate of speed as his sighted friends, although when walking out of water the child's movements are much slower. Apparently the buoyancy of the water gives the blind child the support he needs and provides him with a source of great security and pleasure. The delight on the child's face is well worth the effort parents may have to make in getting to a pool.

We encourage swimming early because it enables the child to *feel* movement he cannot see. He experiences moving separate parts of his body and the different ways he can make them move. The acquisition of muscle control and coordination for swimming must be taught to the blind as well as to the sighted child. However, the blind child may take a bit longer, since he cannot see others swimming.

There is no special technique to teach the blind child how to swim. Anyone can show him how to move his body, arms, and legs in the correct way. The child, of course, must have sufficient language to understand directions. If parents do not feel comfortable in water or are not swimmers, it is best to have someone else teach the child, preferably someone who swims well and enjoys the water, showing no fear.

FINE MOTOR DEVELOPMENT

Fine motor coordination develops gradually, beginning in infancy. At first the infant grasps objects with his palm and gradually learns to use his thumb and the opposing finger. Later he develops a fine pincer grasp, which gives him sufficient coordination to place small pegs, to string small beads, to build with small blocks, etc. He will need the skills as he learns how to button, tie his shoes, and the like. The sighted toddler generally develops this ability quite naturally because he is attracted by and motivated to pick up minute objects, to turn knobs, flick switches, open jars, and pull zippers. The blind toddler may not engage in any of these activities without help. It is tempting to prevent rather than to encourage a toddler to turn knobs and flick on switches, but unless he has this opportunity, he misses valuable training in finger dexterity. Therefore, whenever possible and convenient, the toddler should be encouraged to do all of the things that come so naturally to the sighted toddler. The parent can place his hands on the different objects the child has to turn or pull and go through the motions with him. For example, when going through a door, the parent might suggest to the toddler that he turn the knob; when a jar needs to be opened, the child may be shown how to turn the cap. Turning lights on and off, which all children love to do, is especially exciting for the blind child with light perception. However, although children love to see the lights go on and off, they should not be allowed to become preoccupied with it. A better way of providing this experience is hooking up a switch or knob to a small light set in a box. Such a box, which can easily be made at home, can be great fun for a toddler who has light perception.

Some commercially available toys also enhance fine motor coordination. Others can be made at home: chain locks, slide locks, and locks that need keys can be nailed or attached to a piece of wood. The child can play with it on his lap or on the floor and will have great fun trying the different locks while getting the practice he needs.

Chapter 9

SENSORY DEVELOPMENT

HEARING

All children need to develop good listening skills, but the blind toddler must obtain more information from sound than does his sighted peer. In the section on infants we discussed how the baby differentiates sounds by first identifying his parents' voices. Gradually he learns to recognize sounds and noises and to interpret their meaning. When he learns to creep and walk, he will use his mother's voice to follow her from room to room. At the toddler stage, parents can play several games to enhance listening skills. The parent may call to the child from various parts of the room or home, such as from behind a chair, from within a closet, or from a bathroom. The child can also be encouraged to follow other indoor sounds, for instance the telephone, the vacuum cleaner, a blender, an egg beater, or an electric shaver. However, when the child reaches the source of sound, he will have to be shown what has made it. He should feel it, turn it on, and be shown and told how to use it. If he is not permitted to feel the object and learn its use, he will have no concept of it, although he may be able to name it.

If a child is having difficulty following sounds, it may be because he is being distracted by other noises. Many sighted children, when exposed to more sound and sight than they can tolerate, will tune out and withdraw. The blind child is much more tempted to do this, and so should not be expected to follow a specific sound in a noisy environment until he is older.

Perceiving and following outdoor sounds, such as voices, vehicles, building noises, or animal sounds, can be a bit more difficult, because they do not occur in isolation, and the child does not know their source. Nevertheless, the child will have to learn to listen and to recognize them. The parent will have to verbally explain and describe what the child hears but cannot see.

LANGUAGE

As soon as the sighted child is able to leave crib and playpen and can move beyond the confines of a high chair and the parents' arms, he can explore at close range the things he has looked at and become acquainted with. He can recognize many by name, since sight and sound have blended, one reinforcing the other, to form a mental image. The blind child, too, has heard the words, but he has missed the exposure to and familiarity with an object gained from looking. He has to be helped in this new adventure of exploring and learning and must be offered the words that will help him understand what he "sees" with his hands and his body until touch, sound, and smell combine with the word to form a mental image to be remembered and retrieved at will.

The sighted child sees the people, objects, and actions to which a word refers. Names of members of the family and familiar objects are the first understood and are usually repeated and used by the child after a period of listening and looking. They are followed by an understanding of and eventual use of action words. We must remember that it is an almost universal custom to accompany what is said to a small child with gestures of the hands and facial expressions. The blind child not only misses seeing the objects or activity referred to, he also misses the nonverbal communication that gestures and expressions provide. Many of the gestures the parents would use as they speak to the young child can be transmitted to the blind child by having him feel them or by moving his hands or body to carry them out. Another way to help the child understand the meaning of words is to have a toy doll or animal carry out the action as the child tactually follows it.

Complicating the acquisition of language and speech for the blind child is his inability to observe the speaker's face and the movements of the lips and tongue as he speaks. Fortunately, hearing the sounds and touching the speaker's mouth for a few moments are usually sufficient, and lack of vision does not normally interfere with articulation.

The object basket should now be used daily, and new objects added to the basket—gradually introducing the things the child would see if he could—to further his language acquisition. Small replicas of actual objects can and should be used, since the child has no difficulty whatsoever in transposing size and recognizing the small objects.

Most children repeat words over and over when they begin to talk, practicing the mastery of the new skill as they do in playful repetition of other activities. Once meaning is attached to the word he says and a response obtained, the child often will repeat himself to try out the effect. He has found a new means of controlling his environment and enjoys it, having taken another step in his stride for independence, provided his effort is appropriately met by the adult.

The sighted child, when listening to his mother

speaking, can look at her and, through eye contact, indicate that he has heard. The blind child cannot do this. Instead, he may repeat all or part of what the mother said to indicate that he has heard her (yes, I heard you, this is what you said), showing through this action that he has understood.

As, he cannot see his environment, the child is not motivated to act upon it or in it. As a result, he may enter a room and remain standing still. He has to be told to take off his coat, or else he may remain immobile, not knowing what to do since he does not see what others are doing. Since this response can easily be mistaken for an inability to perform, it is important not to function for him but to help him with verbal encouragement to further his independence and, with it, his self-confidence and emotional growth. Verbal communication helps the child find his way once he has familiarized himself with the surroundings—through touch and sound he can be guided by naming what he passes on his way or what he should avoid. Direct him toward his goal and encourage him to tell where he is.

Although language is the key to intellectual development, care must be taken not to overload the complex system in the brain that processes and generates verbal speech. Sentences should be short and clear and always in reference to the immediate and concrete experience. The child should be allowed time to respond when he tries to communicate. If it can be understood at all, any attempt to communicate, no matter how inaccurately articulated, should not only be acknowledged but should be immediately rewarded with a response. His articulation should not be corrected until language is well established.

The question is often raised whether the words "look" and "see" should be used. We feel very strongly that they should not be avoided. Other people will use them and they will only become more mysterious if the parents do not. Moreover, the young blind child does not know that he is different; he "sees" with his hands. When he is older and aware of being different, blindness will have to be explained and discussed with him.

The difference between "you" and "I" is difficult for all very young children to understand. But for the blind child, it may be a source of confusion conceptually as well as verbally, since he neither sees himself, or even parts of himself, nor the other person. Again, he needs time to assimilate these very difficult concepts, and for several years may confuse "I" and "you" or refer to himself by using his name, as he hears others do. Being unable to see gestures or facial expressions may delay his ability to establish the difference in these words as early as sighted children do.

It is important that sighted people identify themselves to a blind child before talking to him, rather than play guessing games. In this manner, the child does not become preoccupied with trying to figure out who the person might be and instead can concentrate on what is being said.

Many sighted children talk to themselves, and so do many blind children. In fact, blind children may have a greater need to rehearse verbally what they so incompletely experience because of their lack of vision. This need to talk to themselves or to imaginary companions and the satisfaction children derive from it should be respected. If it becomes apparent, however, that the child cannot separate fantasy from reality, he should be reminded of what is real and what is make-believe. This can be done verbally or by games, stressing the difference.

"Where," "why," and "what" are extremely difficult words for all young children to comprehend and respond to. For the blind child, they may present an insurmountable obstacle in his language development unless he is helped by repeated concrete demonstrations. He does not see *where* the toys are—he has to be led to physical contact or follow the voice until he can remember where the sound came from after an object has been dropped or a person has moved away. Also, since the child cannot see the sequence that leads to an event, he may have difficulty understanding cause-and-effect relationships.

The blind child cannot answer his own or other people's questions about *what* someone does unless he has been told or is able to interpret sounds. He will need much more language to think verbally, and by *communicating with himself* solve the many puzzles confronting him most of the time.

The greatest difficulty in the acquisition of language is understanding words referring to what cannot be heard, touched, smelled, or experienced in any direct way—such as colors, the sky, the stars, and the moon. (The sun can be felt by touching the warm window sill or window pane.) Still, these words will have to become part of the blind child's vocabulary; just as sighted children learn the meaning of words they cannot physically experience (such as heaven, love, and God), the blind child will grasp the meaning of much he cannot see.

One of the most effective and usually very enjoyable activities furthering language development is reading to the child. All children enjoy being read to when it is done in a relaxed, nonpressured way and both the parent and the child can enjoy the closeness as well as the story. Since the blind child is missing the visual interpretation (in pictures) of what he hears, care has to be taken in choosing or editing the text to keep it within the child's experience, as well as to explain words or content he might not be familiar with. The blind child, too, will want to hear the same story over and over again. We have found that stories we created ourselves using the child's name, activities, and experiences capture and hold his interest best. The parent, of course, can easily tell about "When Johnny was a baby . . .," "When Johnny went to school . . .," "When Grandma came to visit . . .," "When we went to the supermarket . . . ."

Touch

We have repeatedly suggested that the child, when exploring, be trained to use both hands. In this way, he will feel as much of the details and the outlines as is physically possible. At the toddler stage, the child may resort to mouthing, smelling, using his tongue, or bringing objects close to parts of his face or body. As he becomes skilled in using his hands more efficiently, he will depend less on body contact. Occasionally, an older blind child, in an attempt to know an object better, may fall back upon these earlier patterns. Provided it does not happen frequently and is not likely to become a habit, such methods should be permitted if they help the child "see."

It is during this stage that parents need to help the child use his hands more efficiently by moving them over the object. Just as the sighted toddler sees more and more detail each time he looks at pictures, so does the blind child learn to "see" more each time he feels an object. When the blind child explores something, he needs time to physically cover the entire surface. It is through this experience that he can compare the memory of the tactile exploration and ultimately integrate it into meaningful information. Just as the sighted child looks at the same pictures many times or sees the same objects in his environment each day, so will it be necessary for the blind child to "feel" the same objects repeatedly. It must be remembered that the only part of an object that exists for the blind child is the part that he touches. Therefore, when he is touching an edge of a table top he has no idea what is making it stand unless he explores the legs or the base. The blind child who is given a piece of apple has no way of knowing that the piece given him is a part of the whole unless he is first given the whole apple.

Sometimes parents are disappointed when the child is afraid to touch a new toy they have brought home for him. If the toy makes a noise, the child may have no idea what is making the sound. If the toy does not make a sound, the blind child may still be hesitant to touch it because he cannot see what it is, and his first contact with it must necessarily be a physical one. For some blind children, a verbal description is sufficient; others will be eager to touch it instantly; and still others may be hesitant. The sighted child does not usually have this difficulty because he can observe an unfamiliar object for a long period of time before he becomes comfortable enough with it to want to touch it. If the blind child hesitates to touch a new item, he must be introduced to it gradually by first having the object barely touch his body and then by bringing it closer to him so that he becomes aware of its proximity and is free to explore it whenever he is ready.

All children will try to touch everything they can reach while developing the use of their senses. At first, doing so serves perception, but it may soon develop into uncontrolled and often uncontrollable behavior. The movement of the hand and the grasping of an object then becomes a purpose in itself, and no longer just the means to explore. This is especially so when limits are not set early. The blind child will show similar behavior, though for him the consequences are more serious since touch must remain a highly sensitive tool constantly sharpened to provide information not otherwise available. Nevertheless, tactile exploration must be inhibited in some circumstances because it is inappropriate, for example, when blind children are in the presence of sighted people and touch the person's belongings or the person's body, often making the sighted individual uncomfortable. In such cases, the child will have to be given a verbal description and be satisfied with it.

SMELL

Smell will always contribute to alerting the blind to the presence of people, animals, objects and places, particularly as they move about, and later on as they travel independently. Developing this sense should start early and continue throughout the child's early years.

As we suggested earlier, the child should be exposed to all kinds of scents in the home, drawing his attention to their variety and characteristics. The toddler can be encouraged to identify scents in the home, starting in the kitchen, as well as those outdoors. When taking walks in the park for instance, stop and have the child smell, in addition to touch, the different flowers and shrubs. When in the country, tell the child what the different scents are he smells, such as the barn, the stables, animals, trees, or plants. Not only will it expand his knowledge of the world, but the memory of it will be useful to him as he grows up. When walking in the neighborhood he should be made aware of all the different scents as he passes the bakery shop, shoe store, drug store, florist, etc., and he should be told their names. If possible, he should be taken into each store and be fully exposed to its smells. With this kind of stimulation, some blind children distinguish people by smelling their hands, recognizing the different soaps or perfumes people use. One young blind child who was confused as to which was his scarf, because they all felt alike, smelled all of them and then was able to find his own.

SEVERELY LIMITED VISION

Blind children often have a minimal degree of vision which is so limited that it can easily escape notice. Yet the presence of even severely limited vision may contribute to the development of the child and should be detected as early as possible. It is important for parents to observe the child's reaction and behavior under various light conditions with the following questions in mind:

Does he avoid objects? How big are the objects he avoids and what color? Does he see objects that are only on the floor? Does he lift his head when looking? Does he see things only at head level? Does he appear to see objects from a distance? Does he see better in a certain light? Does he see better in the dark? Does he appear to be disturbed by too bright a light?

If observations suggest the presence of vision, no matter how minimal, it should be brought to the attention of the ophthalmologist. Moreover, the child should be given the opportunity and encouragement to look at objects by moving close to them or by holding them close to his eyes.

The child with severely limited vision is more likely to see brightly colored—especially yellow—slowly moving objects. Yellow against dark blue offers the best contrast. It is helpful therefore to provide color contrasts in the child's environment.

In order to utilize his minimal vision the child may have to tilt his head to find the most effective angle. When this becomes a habit—as it should be—it may disturb the parents. They should realize however, that no matter how minimal the vision it will contribute to the expansion of the child's perception of his world.

with the child during family meals. The child should be told who is at the table: He has no way of knowing who is present or what each is doing unless he is told. Moreover, the child is then participating and is able to keep in touch with his environment. When the parent is preparing the child's plate, she should have him touch it, as well as the dish from which food is being served. When the food is on the plate, the child should feel the food with his fingertips and also smell it.

The blind toddler probably knows how to hold the spoon and bring it to his mouth, but he may still have difficulty scooping and turning the spoon properly. It will help the child if the food is put into a dessert bowl, which makes scooping easier. Scooping and proper turning of the spoon may be difficult for the sighted child as well, since it requires coordination. The blind child has the added disadvantage of neither seeing the food nor observing how others eat. Therefore, it is necessary for an adult to sit next to the child to help him by gently guiding him from his elbow. This will permit the child to exercise the maximum control of his own arm and hand. The child's other hand should keep the bowl from sliding. All toddlers will occasionally pick up food with their fingers. The blind toddler, too, should be permitted to do so. At this stage, the child has probably not learned to place a glass or cup back on the table after he has taken a drink. Again, he needs some assistance in learning to set it down. Parents should tell the child that the glass is on the table or tray and that he should pick it up. If the glass is handed to him in midair, the child will assume it is to be returned into a void. Parents should refrain from taking the glass or cup from the child after he uses it, although he may spill it while setting it down. After the child takes a drink, the parent should be ready to help the child by placing both her hands over his, which are around the cup or glass, and bringing the glass down to the table, showing the child the proper place for it. Pouring small amounts into the child's cup or glass will not only make the glass easier for him to handle, but will be less messy in case of a spill. This is a messy age, but any skill improves with practice. The parent may need to be a bit more patient with the blind child because it takes him longer to develop the skill.

We have stressed that family members should keep in contact with the blind child at the dinner table. When the child is younger, the contact consists of verbalizing what he is doing such as "Jimmy, you are eating," "Jimmy, you are holding a cup." The older child is capable of responding to simple questions, such as "Jimmy, do you want more meat?" It must be remembered that he has no way of knowing to whom the question is directed unless he is first alerted by hearing his name or by being gently touched.

The toddler, blind or sighted, may present problems at meal time by either disliking foods or not wanting to eat at all. The blind child should be handled no differently from the sighted child. Understanding the trouble may help the parent deal with it. The problems surrounding eating habits are not directly related to blindness. Nevertheless, the blind child does not see food that might appeal to a sighted child, nor can he watch others eat—which sometimes stimulates the appetite. Because of his visual impairment parents sometimes permit behavior during meals they would not accept from a sighted child. To ensure that the blind toddler is aware of food that is being served parents should name and comment on the foods they are eating.

TOILET TRAINING

It is generally at the toddler stage that most children become toilet trained. Some sighted children seem almost to train themselves. They have observed family members and one day are ready to use the toilet independently. With the exception of a few accidents thereafter, the process is completed within a very short time. While many children achieve this function easily, some sighted children are unable to do so. We found the same to be true of our blind population. Some parents, feeling anxious about toilet training, pressure their child before he is ready; some children develop fears concerning toilet training for any number of reasons.

Toilet training a blind child and a sighted child follows the same sequence. The difference is that since the blind child cannot see what others are doing, and is therefore unable to imitate it, he has no way of understanding the process until he is shown. Thus, unless an adult makes a conscious effort to explain the proper use of a toilet to him, the child is unlikely to train himself as a sighted child might do.

The sighted toddler observes family members using the bathroom long before he is ready to be toilet trained. The blind child needs the same exposure if he is expected to learn. When the parent goes to the bathroom, the child should accompany him from time to time in order to become accustomed to bathroom activities. He should also feel the toilet and be shown the water that is at the bottom; he should flush the toilet to become familiar with the noise. Later, when he shows signs of being ready to be trained, the parent can go further by having him sit on the toilet. If the child is a boy he can be shown how his father or brother stand to urinate, and also shown the toilet paper, how he must manage clothing, etc. The only way he will make the connection and understand what is expected of him is to feel and hear what he cannot see.

Knowing when the child is ready for toilet training is difficult. A parent can tell that his child is ready when he manifests one or more of the following signals: Does he indicate in some way that he has wet or soiled himself? Is he able to retain urine for at least an hour? Does he show some interest in the use of the toilet? Knowing when the child has soiled or wet his "Pamper" or diaper is a major factor in toilet training. Those of us who have been exposed to young children during this stage have all heard or seen them indicate in some way, whether verbally or through gestures or facial expressions, that they have either wet or soiled themselves. When parents observe these signals, they can be reasonably sure the child is on the way to becoming toilet trained, although it may take several months.

To increase the child's awareness, we have suggested that parents put the child in underpants (not thick training pants) so that when he urinates, he will feel the moisture on his legs. If the child wets more frequently than every hour, he should be returned to the diaper or Pamper. We discourage training pants since they have thick layers of cotton that absorb urine and feel similar to a diaper. On the other hand, underpants, when wet or soiled, are more uncomfortable since they are not absorbent, and thus help the child to become aware of what is happening. Moreover, the parent is prompted to change the child soon after he wets, and the child learns the contrast between dryness and wetness.

A very important factor in toilet training is that the parent remain relaxed. Therefore, when the child wets or soils, it is best to comment, "You have wet your pants. Next time, try to do it in the bathroom. Now let me change you." It is best at this point to have the child feel the wet or soiled pants and, if the floor is wet, the floor as well. Wet clothes should be changed in the bathroom. Before the child receives dry clothing, he should sit on the toilet for a few seconds so he will make the association. We suggest that toddlers wear sneakers during this training period since they can be washed easily.

If the parent knows at what intervals the child is likely to wet or soil, it would be helpful to take him to the bathroom at the expected time. The child should be seated on the toilet for no longer than five minutes.

If the child urinates or has a bowel movement in the

toilet, the mother's tone should be casual. This casual tone is important because if the mother reacts with pleasure when he succeeds, the child might feel like a failure when he doesn't. If the child wets or soils his pants soon after he has sat on the toilet, parents must refrain from reprimanding the child, since doing so may cause anxiety.

Some children have difficulty releasing into the toilet. Many toddlers wet their pants soon after they have been put on the toilet. This is not intentional; the child is attempting to gain control over elimination. Often children may release only a few drops of urine into the toilet, and as soon as they are off release completely. Parents should be encouraged by this sign that the child is well aware of the function of the toilet and that he is trying. All that needs to be said is, "You tried, Jimmy. Maybe next time you will do better." We have found that once the child has released completely into the toilet, he will usually repeat this in the very near future, sometimes the next day.

During this time, the child may have to be taken to the toilet regularly when the parent thinks he may be ready or observes that the child seems uncomfortable. It is not wise to ask the child whether he wants to use the toilet because he may often answer in the negative. It is enough to say, "It is time to go to the bathroom."

As the child becomes accustomed to staying dry, he will eventually express his need to go to the bathroom by using words or gestures. He will later learn to go to the bathroom without announcing it.

Another important factor in preparing the child to be completely independent in using the toilet is to make sure his clothing is as uncomplicated as possible. Snaps, buckles, zippers, and suspenders are all difficult for the young child. Pants with an elastic band at the waist are the easiest for him.

Parents often wonder whether the use of a potty chair or small seat attached to the toilet seat is best. Many parents prefer the small potty seat, and we have no objections to it. We too have used it. However, we have found an occasional child who will not transfer to the big toilet later, and parents are often burdened with carrying the potty seat whenever they leave their home. True, the adult toilet is big and can be frightening to the child, but we have successfully trained many children directly on the big toilet. We found that in a very short time most children learn to straddle the large toilet. A comforting, protective arm around the child helps. The small potty seat is generally reserved for the child who is having a more difficult time.

Training a boy to urinate standing can be difficult because of the height of the toilet. We found that standing the toddler on a small, firm box was adequate. Here again, unless the child is having difficulty, it is best to train him to use the adult's toilet from the beginning. For some boys, transferring from a sitting to a standing position can be difficult. It is best for the father to take the child into the bathroom when he uses it so the child can imitate him.

After the child has been fully toilet trained during the day, he can be trained to control his urine and bowel movements at night. Night training usually occurs quite a bit later than day training. It should be done as persistently as day training. The length of time it takes for a child to be trained to use the toilet at night is usually far shorter than for the day.

There are some very simple procedures that make bowel and bladder control easier during the night: If the amount of liquid given the child during the evening before he goes to sleep is reduced, the child will be less likely to urinate during the night. At this time, the child should no longer be drinking from a bottle. If he is drinking from a bottle during the night or consumes large amounts of liquid before he goes to sleep, it is unreasonable to expect him not to urinate during the night. Just as adults dislike awakening during the night to go to the bathroom, so do children. It also helps to make certain that the child urinates or has a bowel movement before he goes to sleep if such is his habit.

If the child can retain urine and control his bowels for

the entire night, Pampers and diapers should be removed and the child told that he no longer needs diapers. Parents should expect a few accidents during the night and protect the bed adequately. The whole process of toilet training and expecting the child to gain control takes a lot of concentration on the child's part, and he will need time to learn. Parents should exercise patience because it may take as long as six months from the time the child shows signs of readiness until complete control is achieved. Some children do not show signs of readiness until they are much older. If this is the case, causes other than blindness should be investigated.

SOCIAL DEVELOPMENT

The social development of the blind child does not differ from that of his sighted peers. It begins in early infancy, when the bond between parent and child is established. The blind baby needs extra closeness, since he cannot see the parent. The parents must make their presence known, either by direct contact or by their voices. As the normal child grows, his relationships expand to comprise other members of the family, eventually extending to relatives and friends. Since vision plays a major role in this development—mother's face, smiles, and movements, the image that can be recalled—the blind child is in jeopardy. Making body and vocal contact, holding and touching the child, talking to him, singing to him, and indicating the parent's presence will further his emotional and social development.

We suggested earlier that the blind infant be brought to the room in which the parent is working or occupied. Many sighted babies demand this closeness; for the blind baby it is even more important because he cannot see his mother. The blind toddler will continue to need this closeness because, while he has learned to move away from his mother, he has not yet learned to judge how distant she is, and he may be frightened. In addition, he may not have acquired the understanding that when his mother is not present she still exists. The sighted toddler has less difficulty because he has the visual image of his mother in addition to the sound of her voice and the feel of her body. The blind child will not know the mother is present unless she talks to him or touches him.

We suggest that when the toddler is in the same room, the parent bring along objects or playthings for the child to use. In this way, the parent can make intermittent comments to the child, either verbalizing what he is doing or showing him what to do. If the mother has to leave the room, she should tell the child that she is leaving. The sighted child can see her coming and going and moving about. It is unfair to the blind child to leave him without notice. Moreover, the child has to learn that when the mother leaves the room she will return. Because many children at this stage may still be experiencing separation problems, it is often tempting for parents of blind children to leave without warning because it may be too painful to hear the child cry. This may destroy the child's trust.

A great deal of social interaction among people is based on visual communication. Many messages are transferred by looks, smiles, or gestures. Because blind children cannot exchange glances or see those of others, they do not smile as often as sighted children. Therefore, it is important to remember that the parents' smiles must be conveyed through their voices. Similarly, pleasure or displeasure must be expressed verbally.

The best way to teach the blind toddler how to respond to social situations is by including him when visiting relatives or friends. Encourage others to pick him up and to allow the blind child time to respond. It may take him a bit longer to get to know people, since he cannot see them, and he may have to feel their faces. This might be uncomfortable for strangers, but friends and relatives generally understand. If they can be encouraged to play lap games or engage him in any kind of physical activity the child enjoys, it will help the child to build trust in others, as well as being fun for him. If the child has difficulty relating or interacting with adults other than his family, the parents may have to approach the problem slowly. Perhaps the child needs to listen to new voices before he is able to reach out or permit others to interact. Sighted toddlers sometimes react this way in a new situation and withdraw until they feel more comfortable. The blind toddler will need help interacting with other children as well. It is as important to take him to the park as it is for the sighted child. If a park is not convenient, perhaps a baby-sitting play group can be arranged. Some toddlers may not play together, but they do play parallel with each other, and the blind child should not be deprived of this opportunity.

EMOTIONAL DEVELOPMENT

A child's healthy emotional development, whether he is sighted or blind, will depend upon the care, warmth, acceptance, and interaction of one or more adults in his life. The child's feeling of self-worth will be furthered by acceptance and approval of his accomplishments. In our contacts with parents of blind children, we have found that many of them did not know what to expect of their blind child. This made it difficult for them to set goals for their child, often limiting the child's development.

In order for the blind child to develop trust and self-confidence he must be given the opportunity to be independent. At the toddler stage, this independence consists of walking, talking, feeding himself, beginning to develop skills involved in dressing and undressing, and probably being toilet trained. These milestones are important for all children but they are essential to the blind child because they minimize the difference between him and his sighted peers. The feelings parents have about the child are conveyed to the child, blind or sighted, in numerous ways and will affect the child's development. If a parent feels that the child is helpless, he will become helpless. If a parent feels pity, the child will behave to arouse pity. On the other hand, if the parent has trust in the child's ability and expects him to function well, the child will be motivated to meet those expectations and at the same time will develop self-assurance and self-confidence. If demands are set too low, they present no challenge to the child and may hinder his development. If they are set too high, the child will be frustrated. The goals, therefore, must be realistic, taking the child's age, abilities, personality, make-up, strengths, and weaknesses into consideration, as well as his parents' life-style.

If limits are not set, the blind child not only is likely to develop anxiety but later may be unable to set limits for himself, thereby creating problems for everyone. Parents of impaired children often find it difficult to set limits because of pity, guilt, and overprotectiveness. If care is not taken, a blind child will be as difficult as any poorly managed sighted child. The blind child needs all his energy to invest in learning the complexities of living in a sighted world, so he should receive messages firmly, clearly, and lovingly.

Verbalizing feelings is necessary for all children. It is doubly necessary for the blind child because he cannot see others smile, frown, being happy or sad, fearful, looking tired, sleepy, etc. We suggest that in addition to verbalizing how the child feels, parents encourage him to touch their faces or those of siblings or friends experiencing emotions the child cannot see. Parents might try playing games with the blind child, letting him guess what emotions he can recognize from the parent's changing face.

Parents need to prepare the child for any experience that might be unpleasant or painful, such as injections at the doctor, dental work, expected loud noises, etc. The sighted child has time to brace himself for an oncoming event because he can observe the preparations. It is unfair to the blind child to be exposed to unpleasant or even pleasant new experiences without preparation.

Self-care Skills

We often take for granted the sighted child's ability to master skills in dressing, independent feeding, and toilet training. We can be reasonably sure that he will achieve these skills by repeatedly watching and then imitating the activities of others around him. We can, therefore, assume that if we provide the sighted child with a warm, accepting environment and an appropriate model to imitate, he will master all these skills with very little assistance from an adult. We see a similar development in the blind child. He possesses the same ability to imitate, except it will not be achieved through vision but through the actual physical act of doing.

In the section about infants we spoke about arousing the baby's interest in dressing and undressing. By the time the child is a toddler, he will be capable of managing some simple outer clothing such as a hat, a coat, gloves, a sweater, and shoes. Some parents may ask whether this is all too premature for a blind child. It has been our experience that the child does learn to manage simple outer clothing when he is a toddler. We feel it is an appropriate time because the sighted child begins to show interest at this time. Since independence is of utmost importance to the blind child, he will sense his inadequacy when he becomes aware that his sighted peers manage clothing and he does not. Also, if his parents do not expect him to perform, he will have reason to believe he is incapable of doing so. To neglect to develop skills the child is ready to learn may hinder his development.

Removing clothing is easier than getting dressed. Very young babies often learn how to remove a diaper when uncomfortable, and many babies remove shoes and socks without difficulty. Usually the babies do this spontaneously, not for the purpose of undressing. We suggest that the best time to instruct the blind toddler how to remove simple garments is when he is going to bed or coming indoors.

The blind child cannot see others dress or undress and has no idea of when he should do so unless he is taught. The simplest garment to remove is a hat. When the child comes in from outdoors, the parent should tell the child to take his hat off, since he cannot see others doing it. He will also learn that people remove their hats when indoors, and should be told that other family members take their hats off. As he gets older, he will do it automatically and will not need to be reminded. However, if he waits for his parents to remove his clothing, it is usually because he cannot see how others are dressed indoors.

Removing a coat, a button-down sweater, or a jacket is best taught after the clothing has been unbuttoned for him, first sliding the garment slightly off the child's shoulders and then pulling the cuff so the child can reach it when his hands are placed behind his back. Some children often find their own way of removing clothing, or the parents have a method they prefer. Almost any method is acceptable, provided the child can do it without struggling too hard. If there is a zipper, he should be shown how to unzip it by helping him find the metal piece that he needs to pull. A toddler may not be able to unbutton a coat but it would be wise to introduce him to the skill by having him put his hands on the buttons and the buttonholes, and by showing him how the garment separates. Later he will learn how to unbutton. Making him aware of the process is sufficient at this age.

Undressing for bath time or bed can be fun. The parents will find joy in observing not only how the child learns but the child's expression when he participates and succeeds. In the infant section we suggested that the baby go through the motion with the parent as he removes the child's clothing. While he may not have assisted in removing his shirt or undershirt as an infant, he can do it now. Pull his shirt up halfway over his head so that it covers his eyes. Since this is somewhat uncomfortable, he may be motivated to pull it off. Here again, these activities should be accompanied by verbal comments telling the child what he is doing and what is being done for him.

Since a smile cannot be seen, the blind child must hear a smile. Such comments as "Good, Jimmy, you pulled it off over your head" or "You pulled your arm through the sleeve" will not only compliment him but will tell him what he has accomplished. When it is time for his pants to be removed, it is best for the child to be in a standing position. His hands should be placed around the waist of his pants, and he should be told to "pull down." If he does not do it, he will have to be shown. When the child is completely undressed, the clothes that were removed should be placed in their proper places; the child should accompany the parent so that he learns where to put them. Clothes should be put in the same place each time so the child can retrieve them.

Few toddlers, sighted or blind, can dress themselves completely. But many sighted toddlers work diligently at trying to master the art of dressing. It is not uncommon to see a sighted toddler reject assistance, saying "I do it." What we aim for with the children is to instill a similar sense of accomplishment. That is not always simple, since the motivating force that triggers a desire to imitate is sight. The blind child's desire to dress himself must come from a sense of learning and accomplishment he will have to receive from the adults who will teach him. The lessons in these stages will bear fruit when the child feels equal with his sighted peers by also learning to dress himself.

Learning to dress is more difficult than learning to undress, so the process will take longer. The blind child who is handed a shirt in preparation for dressing has no idea where the shirt is coming from, and should go with the parent to collect the clothing he will wear. If it is kept in the drawer, the child should open the drawer, with some help from the parent. In that way, the child not only learns where his clothing is kept, but how heavy the drawer is, how high or low, how hard he has to pull and in which direction he has to bend or reach. It is best to separate the clothing in the drawer; shirts on one side, socks on another. This makes them easier to find and is good training for the future when the child will have to manage for himself. At this age it is difficult for the child to be handed a shirt or undershirt and be expected to slip it on over his head; all he can manage is to pull it down and push his arms through the sleeves. If the toddler is unable to do this, he should be given a few seconds to think about how he is going to solve the task. If the shirt remains half way down over his face and he feels uncomfortable, he may be motivated to pull the shirt down. If the child shows no initiative in pulling his shirt down, it will be necessary to take his hands, place them on the shirt, and manipulate his hands to move the shirt down over his head and his arms through the sleeves.

In teaching the blind child to dress, parents must use their judgment as to which clothes are too difficult for him to manage. To expect the toddler to know a left from a right shoe or to put his socks on with the heel and toe in their proper place is unrealistic. The simplest garments for a child this age to manage are coats, jackets, and hats. Several methods can be used to show him how to dress. For example, lay the coat on a table with the inside facing the child, sleeves spread out and the collar closest to where the child is standing. The child can be shown how to slip both arms into the sleeves, then raise his arms up over his head and push his arms through. Of course, the parent will have to lay out the coat until the child is able to do it for himself.

In getting the child dressed, parents may wonder why he resists wearing gloves, even on a cold winter day. We must remember that the blind child's hands are his eyes, and covering them is like blindfolding a sighted person. If parents are concerned about frostbite, we recommend selecting a coat with pockets in which the child can keep his hands, slipping them out when he needs to "see." Some blind children don't mind wearing gloves, and some manage to slip their gloves on and off. Some blind children may also at times refuse to wear a hat just as some sighted children do. However, the blind child may reject it especially when the hat covers his ears, because it will diminish his ability to hear the sounds he depends on.

The sighted toddler loves to turn faucets and play with water. This is how he learns to regulate the flow of water, as well as the temperature—all new discoveries. The blind toddler loves to do the same, but he must be shown how. Washing his hands after using the toilet is a good start. The same experience the sighted child is exposed to is equally, if not more important for the blind child. The child may need a small box or platform to reach the sink faucet. If paper towels are used, he will need to be shown where to dispose of them. If a cloth towel is used, he will need to be shown how it is hung on a rack. The toddler is capable of learning all this within a few months time and is well on the way to being independent. Again, it will help to keep wastepaper baskets, hampers, etc., within reach and in the same place.

Most toddlers love a bath. However, we have met some children who were frightened of the large tub. In these cases, we put a large basin into the tub. Since the child cannot see the size of the tub, he may need the security of a smaller area.

If that is unsuccessful, the parent may have to get into the tub with the child and hold him. The child might also be frightened of the sound of running water. If so, regulating the flow to a softer sound may help. The child may tolerate the sound as soon as he can feel the water and can control the flow himself.

Chapter 11

PLAY

Play provides the blind child, like the sighted child, the opportunity to grow through imitation and experiments. It stimulates his imagination and intellectual curiosity and teaches him to solve problems. However, for the blind child play will differ in some ways from that of his sighted peers.

While the sighted child may be attracted to a toy or play activity, the blind child may need to be introduced to it through an adult who engages him in play, at least at the beginning. Without intervention, the child is not likely to start playing, at least not until he becomes familiar with the play things, their uses, and where to find them. Nor is the blind toddler likely to "pretend," such as wearing an article of his parents' clothing, as many sighted toddlers may do. The blind child must be shown how it can be fun to imitate daddy by wearing daddy's shoes. The humor and fun a sighted child derives from this can be enjoyed by the blind child as well, but the pretend game needs to be initiated by someone else. It is the responsibility of the parent to provide the necessary opportunities and intervention.

The sighted child usually begins to talk within a short time after he has mastered locomotion. Some children, however, talk before they walk and others talk much later. It is at this stage that the child seems most dependent on vision, and the blind child differs from the sighted toddler in his development. The sighted child exhibits a rapidly growing interest in toys that offer variety in size or shape, such as nests of blocks, graded cups, and form boxes. Since he cannot see them, these toys fail to attract the blind toddler, who prefers his infant toys that make noise. It is not until many months later, usually when language is well advanced, that he will show interest in them. However, with sufficient stimulation and allowance for this interval, the blind child soon makes up for the lost time. For the blind child, language must of necessity play a larger role in the development of concepts and the kind of play which the sighted child is able to acquire earlier through vision.

The blind child's tactile sense at this time of development is not sufficient to help him understand what he is exploring and he needs more advanced language than the sighted child to reach this developmental step, hence the delay.

Nevertheless, these toys should be introduced for very brief periods. Exploring their shapes, sizes, and angles will be a good introduction for later learning. When the child begins to show interest, it is best to offer him sizes with greater contrast before he is introduced to the more subtle gradations. Other sizes can be gradually added until the child is able to arrange an entire set of eight or ten cups in their proper order. We suggest that whatever the child is using be placed on a tray to prevent objects from rolling away and distracting him by requiring him to search for them. If a tray is not available, a shallow cardboard box placed next to the toys will do.

Part of this stage is the development of the child's ability not only to recognize objects he has tactually explored but to begin to perceive similiarities and differences. As the sighted child learns to recognize and match identical pictures (a child may also match without knowing what the picture represents), the blind child learns to match objects. To help him achieve this, the old toy basket will again prove useful.

In order for the child to match objects the parent will need duplicates of at least three common everyday objects with which the child is familiar. Collecting two combs, two cups, and two spoons is the easiest. Three of them, one of each kind, might be placed in a basket. The parent gives a matching one to the child and asks him to "find one like it," until the child has matched all three. Matching different shaped blocks can be done in the same manner.

At this age, children enjoy building towers, but most of all they like to knock them down. Blind children also enjoy this activity. Graded cups turned upside down or small cans and cereal boxes may be used. The variety of objects used in building a tower gives a blind child another opportunity to feel different weights, sizes, heights, and shapes. While this is equally important for the sighted child, the blind child needs the concrete experience of exploring the objects' single parts, which the sighted child can grasp from looking. In showing a child how to build a tower, the adult must build several first. Then both hands of the child should feel the pieces and how they rest one on top of another. Only then will the blind child know what a tower is like. When the child is ready to build, it is best for him to use both hands to stack the objects. The toddler's coordination will not be fully developed, but he will be able to build a tower although the alignment may be off.

Some time during the toddler stage, when the child is walking independently and has more language, he begins to show interest in the use of interlocking toys and fitting things together. Some commercially made toys are available in different sizes, such as Lego blocks and bristle blocks. The

Lego sets are notched so that they fit together. They come in all sizes—the larger ones are best at this time. The bristle blocks are designed so that they stick when pressed together. Since the blind child has no idea of what can be done with these toys, he will have to be introduced to the finished product first. Therefore, the parents will have to create a simple design initially, have the child feel it with both hands, take it apart, and then help the child rebuild it. In that way, the blind child will understand what he is doing.

Snap beads can be purchased in almost any dime store at a minimal cost. These plastic beads simply snap together to form a string or rope. It is best to snap several beads together for the child first and have him feel the entire row so that he knows what it looks like. After he runs his hands along the row of beads, he can help pull them apart, thus learning the process. To show him how they snap together, the parent should have him hold one bead in each hand and show him how they snap together.

Stringing beads can be taught in a similar manner, but difficulty sometimes arises because the string slips away. It will help to take the end of the string and attach it to the table where the child is working with a piece of tape, thereby making it more accessible. If the threading end of the string is too short and difficult to manage, it can be lengthened by rolling scotch tape around the top three inches of the string. Children who have an especially difficult time can start off with pipe cleaners instead of string.

In the section about infants we advised parents to try out any toys they buy with their eyes closed before purchasing them. This will give parents a better perspective not only of how the blind child "sees" toys but also whether the toys will be easily managed by the child and will not frustrate him. When parents test these toys with their eyes closed, they must remember that their frame of reference is quite different from that of the child, since they have actually seen the toy first. They must also keep in mind that the child's fine motor skills are still rather limited, so the toys should be fairly simple to manipulate.

Form boxes which are sold commercially are enjoyable and educational for all children. The sighted child generally begins using them by trial and error. That is, he inserts one block into a hole and if it does not fit, tries another one until he finds the correct one. For the blind child the approach must necessarily be different. It is best to begin by covering all the holes with tape, leaving only the round and square holes, and moving his fingers inside the holes so he can feel the difference. The corresponding blocks should be placed in his hands, named, and he should be shown how they fit into the holes. Once the child places them into the correct space, in order to ensure that he does not remember the position of each hole rather than the shape, the box should be turned around. When the child learns the round and square shapes, the others can be introduced one at a time.

Similar toys on the market have very odd-shaped blocks. With the blind child, particularly in the early years, it is best to avoid shapes that are unusual. A homemade form box can also be made from a shoe box and empty spools of thread. A hole the size of the spool can be cut out of the lid of the box. If a parent has square blocks, a square hole can be added to the lid of the shoe box. Although a few blind children use and may enjoy simple preschool wooden puzzles, most children have difficulty recognizing their representations.

Ball playing is fun for all children. To help the blind child learn how to use and enjoy a ball, parents may need specific directions. First show the child how the ball rolls by placing his hand on it, with the adult's hand over the child's hand, letting him feel the movement of the rolling ball. The child can be shown how to roll the ball to someone while sitting with his legs far apart so that when it is rolled back to him he can easily retrieve it. However, he should be shown the very beginning skill of how a ball can be thrown: The parent places his hand on the child's hand that is holding the ball and guides the child's arm in a throwing movement.

In practicing the skill of throwing a ball, the parent can have the child throw the ball at a target such as a cardboard box with a bell attached that the parent can ring intermittently. This will teach the child how to listen for the sound and find the direction in which to throw the ball. He might be asked to throw the ball to someone calling him. This will help him develop the skill of listening to a particular sound coming from a particular direction. It may take several trials before the child learns how to throw a ball in the direction of the sound.

Occasionally, it is possible to find a ball that has a beeping sound or a bell inside that gives a clue to which direction it is going. The bell also allows the child to find the ball when it has dropped, so that he will not be frustrated when it rolls away. One parent gave us the idea of attaching a string to a ball, so when the child throws it he can easily retrieve it. However, this should be used for only a limited time, and the child should learn to retrieve the ball by listening for its bounce and estimating where the ball has fallen and where to reach for it. The use of balls will remain a source of joy and an educational experience throughout childhood.

We mentioned in the infant section that blind children who have light perception are especially fond of playing with lights. We suggested connecting a switch to a box with a light inside. Now that the child is older, other attachments can be added or made separately, such as a light dimmer, a switch that when turned on makes a bell ring, or a pull chain that will turn on the light, all inside the box. These devices may be difficult to make but students in a neighborhood vocational school perhaps can help make them under the supervision of a high school teacher. We have had some excellent toys made by sighted high school students.

We have found that blind children do not particularly enjoy pull-toys. They do not seem to receive that much pleasure from them despite the fact that they make a tinkling sound when they are pulled. However, most blind children do seem to enjoy larger toys on wheels, such as a doll carriage, a walker, or any other toy that can be pushed. These toys are particularly useful because they have a protective quality, shielding the child when he bumps into a wall or into furniture. A kiddie car is another toy a toddler can learn to use and enjoy. Again, he will have to be shown how to push with his feet.

Now that the child moves about, games such as "hide and seek" will be helpful in teaching him where to find you. Moreover, it will teach the child that although the mother is silent, she is still present. It will also teach the meaning of "hiding" although he cannot differentiate between visible and invisible. It is interesting how quickly the child will learn this concept and receive as much enjoyment from the game as a sighted child does.

Letting a child go barefoot for a while sometime during the course of the day will enable him to feel rugs, floors, and different textures of floor coverings that he may not otherwise be aware of. Allowing him to go barefoot outdoors in warm weather is also recommended. It is the only way he will be aware of and experience different surfaces, such as grass, sand, and gravel.

A large fenced in area outdoors will give the child the freedom his playpen had given him earlier. Once the child knows the boundaries of the area and is familiar enough with trees, flowerbeds, or a sand box so that they are no longer obstacles, he will feel free and secure. A tinkling chime over the doorway to the house may help the child orient himself and become independent enough to go back to his mother when he needs her.

The blind child must be shown the different ways he can play with water. He might be placed at the sink or in the bathtub and be provided with various types of objects, such as containers, squeeze bottles, a watering can, basting syringes, sponges, plastic cups, or eyedroppers—no more than two or three at a time. The parents will have to show the child how they are used by putting their hands over the child's hand and going through the appropriate movement. At the same time, the parents should comment on what is happening, for example, that the water is pouring out of the spout, "you are squeezing water out," "the cup is being filled," or "the water is being sprinkled." Verbalizing these actions for the child is necessary to help him to understand what he is doing and to remember it more easily. We cannot stress strongly enough the importance of speech accompanying every activity the child is involved in, describing to him what he would see if he had vision.

The blind child should be taken to parks and playgrounds. Blind children can and should enjoy the swing, slide, sand box, jungle gym, and other outdoor play equipment that sighted children his age use and enjoy.

Once the child becomes familiar with a swing he should learn to pump on his own. He should be able to climb his way up the slide, come down, and then find his way back to the steps of the slide. He should learn to climb the monkey bars by himself, to push himself up and down on the seesaw, etc. This will give him the opportunity to come into contact with other children.

Many parents report that their blind children enjoy spending long periods listening to records, cassettes, or the radio. While these forms of listening can be enjoyable, prolonged use of them should be avoided. Since the child has no visual attraction, he may become totally absorbed in the musical sounds. This could encourage passivity and sometimes even loss of touch with the environment. It is therefore recommended that records be appropriate for the child's interest and his level of comprehension and that they encourage the child to participate by singing along, playing an instrument, "dancing" to the music, etc. Some records are particularly pleasing to blind children because they involve different kinds of familiar sounds such as sounds "in the home," "in the city," "in the country," and "animal sounds."

Most sighted toddlers are impatient to be allowed to

pour liquid as they watch their cups and glasses being filled. They quickly learn to do it and soon gain sufficient coordination and control to avoid spilling much of the time. Blind children, too, need the experience, not only because it provides fun and fills a need for independence, but also because in the course of learning to pour, the child utilizes sensations that will be useful to him in many other ways. The empty glass or cup is lighter than one containing liquid. He will learn the relationship of the position of the container or pitcher to the cup or glass; the lighter it is, the more he has to tilt it. He will also use the changes in sound; he learns to measure fullness by dipping his finger to the level of the liquid, using the sensation of moisture as his guide.

To help the child develop these skills and to increase his enjoyment, dry pourable materials to play with such as rice, split peas, elbow macaroni, beans, and sugar can be used. Any one of them can be poured into containers of varying sizes such as measuring cups or pitchers. After fingering, the child can pour whatever he is using from one container into another, or he may be shown how to fill a cup or container by using spoonfuls, checking the increasing amount by touch and weight. As soon as the child has developed some skills in pouring dry materials he should be allowed to experiment pouring water. Since he cannot see that he has spilled, he should be encouraged to touch the wet surfaces to make him aware of the consequences. Later, when he is more adept, he should be taught to wipe up spilled liquid. It would be helpful to put everything on a tray so that the spilled liquid remains contained.

Another educational part of play is putting toys away. Not only is it a lesson in taking care of possessions, but it also enables the child to learn where things belong so that he can retrieve them independently. A sighted child will see where his toys are even when they are not in the correct place. The blind child needs to learn the location of each toy, and it is essential when parents set up their children's room that the toys be placed on a shelf the child can reach and that each toy have a special place. Since a large number of toys can be confusing to the blind child, as well as to the sighted child, it is recommended that no more than six or seven toys be taken out at any given time. When a toy is replaced by another one, the child should help the parent put it away so he will learn where it can be found. A rotation of toys helps develop interest in the things the child owns. Having the child put the toys away gives him additional opportunity to get around in the house on his own. If a child seems to have difficulty locating a toy, the parent should give the child verbal directions rather than handing him the toy. When giving directions to a blind child, parents should begin by referring to the child's own body, for example, that the ball is on the shelf *above your knee*, the puzzle on top of the shelf *above your head*, bend down, you can find the peg *by your foot*.

Once the child has learned to ride a kiddie car, a tricycle can be introduced. Some toddlers, whether sighted or blind, learn to ride a tricycle without difficulty; others need more time. The blind toddler should be encouraged to explore the entire tricycle. Also, the child should be helped onto the tricycle rather than placed on the seat so that he will learn how to position his own body.

Tricycles are useful in developing gross motor coordination. They also provide the child with a means of moving from one place to another in a fast and safe manner. The tricycle itself protects the child, since the front wheel will hit obstacles first. Children also can enjoy riding tricycles in a hall area where they can identify the location of the walls by the echoes of their voices as they approach. In this way they learn how to estimate the distance between themselves and a wall and how to avoid bumping into it. Blind children might also be encouraged to follow the sound of a child in front who might be ringing a bell or singing a song as he rides his own tricycle. Since the child cannot see how the pedals move on the tricycle, he will have to be shown how to use them. Once he has learned, he will become as adept in riding a tricycle as any sighted child.

The blind toddler, like his sighted contemporary, is a joy to watch. The fact that he needs somewhat more supervision and presents more of a challenge to the parents' ingenuity in providing the necessary stimulation and intervention can make helping his development even more rewarding.

All children sense their own growth and know when they are being helped. The blind child's beaming face and his growing self-confidence are ample proof of this.

Part III

THE YOUNG CHILD:
FROM THREE TO FIVE YEARS

Chapter 12

LANGUAGE

Although the infant is dependent on his environment to have his needs taken care of, once on his feet the toddler strives for independence and explores his surroundings. At the end of the toddler stage, the blind child, who may have missed some of the developmental progression earlier as a result of his lack of vision, will proceed at an accelerated pace to reach and keep step with his sighted peers. We should expect, therefore, that the young blind child will become more curious about strangers, more interested in participating in the social give and take, and able to understand and use verbal language. As a result, he will become less shy with strangers, show more curiosity about people and things, partly by listening and hearing about them, partly by exploring them with his hands.

The young child prefers to "do it himself," within his physical capability and sometimes beyond. The young blind child should, therefore, be offered every opportunity to fill this need within the limits of safety. He is now becoming possessive and, like his sighted contemporary, claims "it is mine." To avoid the unnecessary frustration and anger common in all children at this age, the young child should know where he can find his toys and favorite objects. His play will now be accompanied by talking and may soon be addressed to an imaginary companion; imagination and make believe will play a greater part. Since he cannot perceive or check visually what is real, he should be made aware of and helped to distinguish between fantasy and reality.

The young blind child, like the sighted child, is interested in listening to stories. While pictures help the sighted child understand the words read to him, the blind child is totally dependent on what he hears. Thus, it is important to start with short stories about familiar events and to explain and describe what the child misses by not being able to look at illustrations.

This is the time for intense, rapid intellectual development to which the development of language contributes in a large degree. However, care must be taken not to overstimulate the child and to make sure he understands what is said to him. The fact that he repeats what he hears is not always proof of comprehension or acknowledgement, and when the young child repeats most of what he hears, without acting upon it, his language development should be watched. By the same token, when the young blind child fails to use words, phrases, and sentences and does not have the words for most of what he wants to convey, causes other than blindness may be responsible.

For the young blind child, the command of language— that is, his ability to understand and use spoken words—will not only determine his ability to communicate with others and with himself, but will remain his closest link with the world he cannot see. Verbal description will have to replace sight; words will have to serve as anchors for memory of fleeting, tactile impressions and enable him to retrieve them.

The ability and opportunity to express feelings are important for all children. The young blind child depends more on verbal communication of feelings since he misses eye contact and does not see facial expressions and body movements. He also must be made aware that his feelings are recognized and be told how others feel.

Since young blind children are not motivated to look at a speaking person, most do not raise their heads or turn their faces toward the speaker. This discourages communication, since it seems to the sighted person as though the blind child is neither listening to nor addressing him. It is therefore necessary to gently turn the child's face up and toward the speaker or listener until this posture has become a habit. The sighted child also often has to be reminded to look at the person to whom he speaks, even though he is visually motivated to do so.

Chapter 13

ADVANCED MOTOR DEVELOPMENT

GROSS MOTOR DEVELOPMENT, MOBILITY, AND ORIENTATION

Most sighted children experiment with movement because they can see their own bodies in motion, as well as others' whom they imitate. It is not uncommon for the sighted child to call his mother to watch while he walks on his knees, tumbles, rolls, cat-walks, stands on one leg, jumps off steps, balances a book on his head, or even tries to stand on his head. He shows his delight at all these accomplishments. The child who cannot see, is not likely to engage in any of these activities. He has the same ability to perform and enjoy them, but he must be shown how. Therefore, the parent may have to think back to his own childhood or observe children as they engage in these activities, which many children refer to as "doing tricks." It is sometimes difficult to show the child different positions because his hands cannot feel the adult's entire body in motion. The best way is for the parent to get into a specific position, and to let the child follow the contour with his hands. If the child has difficulty, the parent might position the child's body for him. It is most helpful to have the child follow the outline of the adult's body first, because it will give him some idea of what he is to imitate.

Parents can also engage children in such exercises as push-ups and knee bends, touching the toes, stretching the arms in various directions, lying on the floor with legs up at a right angle and lowering them slowly, and moving separate parts of the body independently, such as one shoulder, one leg, etc.

Unlike the sighted child, the blind child should not be expected to spontaneously acquire words indicating space, or the meaning of words such as on top of, at the bottom, in front, at the back and sides without being taught. There are several games that can be played with blind children that facilitate learning, such as Simon Says, Hoky Poky, May I?, Looby Loo, and Follow the Leader. They should be presented to the child in the spirit of fun, not as a drill.

Outdoor activities are equally important, especially in developing large-muscle skills. Sighted children on the playground are constantly moving, exploring the equipment, and trying to learn new skills. A three-year-old might be riding a tricycle, a four-year-old climbing a jungle gym or using the big slide, the five-year-old might try climbing a tree or perhaps walking along a ledge. They are all having fun, expending energy, learning how to balance their bodies and coordinate their large muscles. The sighted child is motivated not only because he sees the equipment, its size, shape, and height, but because he is also likely to see other children using them. The blind child can enjoy the same challenges and can be just as successful. He, too, needs to expend energy, have fun, and master these skills. However, he must be shown where the equipment is, how to use it, and how to use his body. Before the child attempts to use the equipment, he should be given a verbal description of the apparatus and what he can do with it. He should also be encouraged to touch as much of it as possible. For example, if a parent chooses the jungle gym, she might let the child feel the lower bars, have him walk under them if possible, have him feel the bars that are higher and then describe the bars up higher that he can hold onto and climb. The child must be reassured by the parent that she will watch, and she will have to keep calling to him to assure him of her presence. If other children are using the jungle gym, the child should be told so, and since the blind child cannot see the enjoyment on the others children's faces, the parent must convey enjoyment and enthusiasm through her voice. It is best to have the child engage in these activities gradually: allow the child to climb on two rungs the first time; once he feels comfortable at that height, he can be allowed to climb higher. Once he has experienced success and joy, he will be eager to try other equipment.

If the child is in a playground where large wooden blocks are available, they can be used to great advantage by placing them a few inches apart, either in a straight row or in a circle. The child can be shown how to walk on each block and find the next one with his foot. If he succeeds when the blocks are a few inches apart, they can be spaced further away until the child must take a wide step to reach the next block. This is an excellent game for learning to judge distances.

Roller skating is an activity most children enjoy. The blind child is no exception. However, because it requires balancing, it is best to give the child one skate at first. He will be eager to try both as soon as he feels secure on one. Holding onto a handrail gives the child support. If that is not available, holding an adult's hand will suffice. The child will soon learn to put the skates on and remove them by himself.

The majority of blind children are unable to run with the same speed and efficiency as their sighted peers. Even when they are shown the movements involved using a doll or human model, most blind children seem to have difficulty running and do not swing their arms normally. However, running can be facilitated by taking the child's hand and running along with him, which most blind children seem to enjoy very much. Also, a rope can be strung between two points, indoors or outdoors, which the child can hold onto as he runs. When the child has sufficient practice with this support, a large open space, free of obstacles, should be made available to him where he can practice.

As soon as the child is moving about freely and is able to use landmarks to orient himself when he loses his way, parents should make certain that he knows the entire room well by having him point to various areas and objects in the room, such as a doorway, window, couch, fireplace, or table. Some blind children can do this very well, while some need a point of reference, for instance, an explanation that they are standing by a certain piece of furniture or facing the kitchen. Some may have more difficulty, and should be returned to trailing, which will give them a better mental image of the room. Some blind children are better oriented than others because of their better sense of direction and previous training.

The next step in orientation is learning concepts such as "facing each other," "side by side," and "back to back." It is best to begin with two dolls, which the child can position in various ways by feeling their faces and backs. When the child learns to do this, he should practice with an adult or another child.

More difficult is teaching the child quarter turns, half turns, and full circles. Again, using a doll will help. The child can position the doll in the center of a circle that has four markers spaced at 90 degree marks to form a full circle. He can turn the doll to face each marker until it has completed the circle. After he has learned how to move the doll, he can learn to move himself while standing in a circle with markers while an adult calls to him from each 90 degree point until the child has turned fully. Having the child touch the four markers with his foot helps him feel the quarter turns as he swings his legs to find the markers.

Walking a straight line may be equally difficult for the child. He can be helped by first demonstrating straightness by pasting a pipe cleaner on a sheet of paper and having the child run his fingers along this straight line. Another pipe cleaner can be pasted in a curved line next to the straight one and the difference pointed out to the child. The idea of straight and curved lines can also be demonstrated in clay where he can follow a straight or curved groove. After the child has done this he should be encouraged to connect two points by moving his fingers without a guide. The markers can be two pieces of scotch tape placed about eight inches apart. In other words, he has to find the first piece of scotch tape and then move his fingers either horizontally or vertically to the other piece of scotch tape in a straight line (Figure 13-1).

A straight line may further be taught by having the child walk between two railings, which can be made of wire,

Figure 13-1.

rope, or two long bars, two feet apart, at the child's waist level. The child should start at one end and try to walk without touching the rails. If he veers, he will feel the rail and know he is not walking a straight line. At this age, it will suffice if the child learns how his body feels when veering. Some children learn to walk a straight line for a distance of about 10 to 15 feet without guide rails or sound cues. Beyond that and without cues, it is an unrealistic expectation for the young blind child.

We have never ceased to be amazed how well some blind children move from one point to another avoiding obstacles without sound cues. (One would expect this from children who have light perception.) These are children who, in a familiar environment, find their way without difficulty. We assume these children measure distance by the time elapsed from their starting point to their destination. When they are asked how they find their way, they respond simply, "I just know." Reports from blind adults whose vision was restored indicate that they had difficulty adjusting to the rhythm of walking because the time it took them to walk from one point to another, when blind, was different. Therefore, since some blind children need more practice than others, we suggest that parents occasionally encourage their blind child to count when going from one place to another in order to emphasize the time it takes.

Learning to distinguish left from right is difficult for all young children. However, blind children are more dependent on verbal directions and other aids and should receive help. The first step, of course, is the awareness of left or right on their own body. If a child has difficulty remembering them it may help to tie a ribbon to one of his wrists, noting that it is either the right or left. Playing games that involve putting the right hand in or out, such as Looby Loo or Hoky Poky, may help the child to learn this differentiation.

It is sometimes tempting to simply take the child by the hand and lead him to his destination, but a blind child that is led is being deprived of the opportunity to acquire mobility and is denied "seeing" the environment. The time invested in teaching a child how to find his way will ultimately *save* time and the child's sense of achievement and independence will be well worth the effort. The young child can be taught to move from one place to another independently in an area where he is expected to spend a great deal of time, such as in the home, in school, or possibly in the home of a relative or friend.

TRAILING

We suggested earlier that the toddler be introduced to the trailing method of mobility. As a toddler, the back of his hand kept contact with the wall as he moved along. Now he must learn that his hand should be pointing slightly downward, to avoid getting his fingers caught in openings, while his other hand should be held in front of his body at waist level and bent at the elbow. Thus, one hand moves along the wall while the other hand protects the upper part of the body (Figure 13-2).

Figure 13-2.   Trailing.

The parent will have to begin by placing the child at a starting point, to which the child will later return. It will be necessary for him to remember what he is passing, but since it is too difficult for him to remember everything he touches and retain the sequence, each point should be taught gradually. For example, if on the way to the outdoor area the child's hand touches a door, a wall, a water fountain, or a recessed wall, he should be expected to remember only three different points in the order he will pass them. Each day, the child should begin at the same starting point and remember one more reference point, thereby getting closer to his destination. Some children can learn to travel 100 feet or so within a few days, while others take longer to learn to do so. After the parent has taken the child on a mobility "trip," it is best to verbally review with the child what he has passed and touched and in what order, to reinforce the child's memory. Mobility should be taught in a quiet area so he can concentrate without being distracted. When a child is taught mobility in a room or hall he must be given the opportunity to feel the entire room and the objects in it in order to gain as complete an impression as possible of the area and a sense of the spatial relationships. When the child has learned to find his way, he should be sent on short errands, with some supervision, to allow him to experience and enjoy this newly acquired independence.

Traveling independently extends to the outdoors as well, although outside mobility will not be accomplished until later. In the meantime, it is important to teach him how to combine what he hears, touches, and smells into meaningful information. Later, more formal and more complex mobility training with the use of a cane or dog will be introduced.

The child should be taken into the street with only one specific goal in mind. For example, on one trip the child may be taken out only to listen and point to the direction of the traffic; on another trip only to listen to a variety of sounds and become aware of them, for example traffic stopping or the faint clicking of the traffic light as it changes. Another day the sole purpose of the trip may be to feel all the buildings in a row. This trip might be followed up later with block building to resemble a street. Another venture could be a visit to the stores within a block or so to guess what they sell. If the child lives in the country, walks can be taken with other goals in mind—pointing out landmarks such as different tree smells or paths with their different ground surfaces. These trips should be frequent enough for the child to remember.

If a parent feels the child is ready, he can be taught to walk by himself from one place to another outdoors—for example, visiting a friend or relative a few houses away. The method used would be similar to the indoor mobility lesson of trailing and using landmarks, gradually adding two or three landmarks each time.

We have been able to teach four and five year old blind children to travel from the seventh floor of a building to the street and down half a block by having them trailing walls, touching buildings, and remembering all the landmarks in the order they touch them. It is important for a child to recall verbally what he passed before and after he has traveled the distance. This training was not initiated for the purpose of independent traveling at this young age, but merely as preparation for later learning. It proved that the children were able to attend, remember, and most of all, enjoy the preparation. This is not as unusual as it may appear because sighted children this age generally know the direction they have to travel to visit a friend or go to a candy store nearby.

Some sighted people often wonder how blind adults can perceive obstacles in their path before they come in contact with them. The reason is that blind people have become aware of subtle changes in sound echoes coming from objects within close proximity. The skill in listening for these changes can be taught to children. This is best accomplished by setting up a room with objects randomly placed in the child's path. Large cardboard boxes serve the purpose best since they will not hurt the child. The child can learn to hear the sound echoes bouncing off the boxes when he claps his hands or stamps his feet as he moves along. If the child suddenly stops or avoids the obstacles, he obviously is receiving the sound echo although he may not be aware of it. If this is the case, he should be asked what made him stop or avoid the object, thus making him aware of what he is experiencing.

These sound echoes are also used by blind children in a new environment. It is not unusual to see a child tapping his feet, clapping his hands, or making sounds in an effort to gain information about the feeling and size of a room and its contents. This should not be discouraged, if kept within reasonable limits. It is for this reason that we recommend the child wear leather soles on his shoes, since rubber soles will give him no sound clues. When the child was first learning to walk, we suggested sneakers for better gripping, but this is no longer necessary.

SIGHTED-GUIDE TECHNIQUE

On many occasions, the blind child should not be expected to trail on his own and the parent should take the child to his destination without allowing him the benefit of "seeing his environment." At these times, the sighted-guide technique should be used. This involves having the child walk half a step in back of the parent, and holding the forearm of the adult with the palm of his hand (Figure 13-3). In this way, the sighted adult guides the blind child by protecting him with his body. If the child cannot reach the forearm of the adult this technique should nonetheless be used by having the child hold the parent at the lower arm or wrist, whichever is more comfortable. Children whose

Figure 13-3.   Sighted-guide technique.

hands are held tend to be pulled instead of being allowed to follow the cues they would receive from perceiving the movement of the body of the adult, especially when the adult steps up, down, turns a corner, or stops. This sighted-guide technique has many advantages: it is safer, and will give the child a feeling of independent walking, as well as allowing others to guide the child.

FINE MOTOR DEVELOPMENT

In previous sections of this book, we discussed the importance of hand coordination. The older child should be encouraged to put the key into the lock and open the door, and to join daddy when he is going to use simple safe tools around the house. He should be shown how tools are used and allowed to try them. He can now open jars of various sizes. If adhesive tape is being used, he should be asked to try to use it, too. He might enjoy practicing by buttoning his parents' coats sometimes instead of just his own.

Other activities that the child will enjoy at this age and that will enhance his fine motor coordination include picking up one large lima bean from a four ounce container filled with beans and gently letting it drop into an empty container, or scooping each bean with a small spoon that holds only one bean at a time.

Chapter 14

GROWING UP

Grooming

Just as it is important for the sighted child to take care of his body, so it is for the blind child, although he needs more training to do so. The parent may begin by teaching the child how to brush his teeth, wash his hands and face, comb or brush his hair, and adjust his clothing properly. Learning to turn water on and off, feeling for the hot and cold water, and putting the stopper in the sink are all learned quickly and simply by most blind children. Many of them are quite adept at those skills by this age. The child may need a small box to step on to reach the basin or taps. Towels, soap, and wastepaper baskets should all be within his reach. Some parents teach the child to use a washcloth, showing him how to wet the cloth, rub the soap on it, and bring it to his face. He must also be shown how to wring it out and hang it on a rack.

Brushing teeth is also easily learned, but it is best begun by having the child explore the toothbrush without wetting it or putting toothpaste on it. He then should unscrew the cap of the toothpaste tube and squeeze out a small amount of toothpaste, which he can measure with his fingers. Children love to squeeze the toothpaste. It should be a very small amount at first, or he may be overwhelmed by the paste in his mouth. Learning to put everything away is also important, so the child will know where to find his toothbrush the next time because he has put things where they belong.

Sighted children learning how to comb their hair improve with practice. The blind child will also learn this but he has to feel the part in his hair and know which way he has to comb it. This is difficult since the child must learn good grooming without seeing himself or others. The parent should teach these skills while standing behind the child. Directing him from this position is more natural for both the parent and the child. At first, the mother may have to place her hand over the child's hand, holding the brush or comb. But as the child gains better control, she can guide him from the elbow until no guidance is needed. The child can then check by touch whether his hair is parted or combed correctly, touching the back, sides, and front, and will gradually learn when he has done it right.

DRESSING AND UNDRESSING

During the toddler stage, the blind child should have had a great deal of practice in removing his clothing, with only some assistance from his parents. Now the child should be able to manage undressing completely and should also be able to collect all his soiled clothes and place them where they belong. Learning to dress is more difficult. As a toddler, he learned to put on clothing that was easy to handle, such as a coat, sweater, or a hat, and he was able to assist his parents while being completely dressed. Now, he should be able to dress himself completely, except for some help with buttoning and lacing.

In order for the child to select his clothing and dress himself, the clothes must be easily accessible and kept in an orderly manner, and he must know in which order they are worn. Hooks and closet rods for his clothing should be low enough for him to reach. Clothes that are hung on a hook should have large size loops sewn at the neck so he can be assured success and avoid frustration when hanging them up. Clothes in the drawer should be organized so the child knows where to find them. He will learn by counting drawers where specific clothing is kept. If the child has been taught to put clothes away, it will be simple for him to find them. When the parent has to make changes and rearrange things, the child should help, so that he knows what is happening. Most clothing can be recognized by the texture or some other identification that is on the garment, such as buttons, rick-rack trim, or a collar. The inside of clothing can be recognized by the seams. If an article of clothing is difficult to recognize, a mark of identification, such as a small special button, can be sewn on. Since the coordination of clothing is difficult for all children, this task presents even more difficulty for the blind child. However, he will learn by textural combinations, for example, that the *cotton* shirt goes with the *corduroy* pants. To simplify matters of dressing, it is best to avoid buying the child clothing of similar textures or identical styles.

Children will be curious about color because they will hear references to it. The child can learn that certain colors go with some and not others and parents can make reference to these combinations, such as "your blue shirt with the collar goes with your white cotton pants."

Winter clothing such as snow pants and jackets can be difficult for all children to handle because they sometimes have cumbersome linings and narrow cuffs. When parents are selecting these items, they should buy practical, easy to manage clothing. Boots are particularly difficult, even more so if the child is wearing rubber soled shoes. Pulling boots on can be made easier by giving the child plastic bags to slip over his shoes. The plastic allows the foot to slip into the boot easily.

Whenever possible, the child should select the clothes he wants to wear. If he insists on wearing an inappropriate garment, however, such as a sleeveless top in January, parents should exhibit the same kind of firmness they would with a sighted child. Since the child cannot see how others are dressed, this can become more of a problem. In such instances, giving the child a choice among a few appropriate garments might help. In this way, whatever choice the child makes will be agreeable to the parents.

A great amount of learning takes place when a child is expected to select and collect his own clothes, remember the textures and combinations, and then dress himself. He must first of all know where to find the clothing; then he will have to remember that his underpants may be in the top drawer and perhaps his socks in the drawer below. He will have to know how to move his body and in which direction to reach or bend. After he collects his underwear and socks, he will have to remember where his pants, shirts, and shoes are kept. When choosing his pants and shirt, he will have to remember the combinations he has been taught. Learning to pair combinations, whether they be textures or tags, enhances tactile sensitivity. Moreover, practice will increase his self-confidence, in addition to making him feel like one of his sighted peers. When the child has completed a task, parents must not forget to compliment him, since he cannot see the smile of approval on their faces or the result in the mirror.

Learning to zip, button, lace, etc., requires dexterity. Like the sighted child, the blind child will need practice. Therefore, whenever the opportunity arises, the blind child should be shown how to button, unbutton, zip, lace, snap, hook, buckle, and tie. Before any of these skills are taught, we assume the child is capable of putting garments on and taking them off. Some children might enjoy practicing on a large doll. Special frames are commercially available that have buckles, zippers, and buttons to practice on. The larger any one of the fasteners is, the easier it is for the child to learn to use it. Frames can also be made at home, with two pieces of fabric attached to a board, one with large buttons, another with buckles, and still another with large zippers.

When the child is being taught how to manipulate fasteners, parents should stand behind him and move his hands, describing the different movements; for example, "hold the button in this hand while you find the button hole with the other; keep your finger in the hole; now push the button into the hole and pull it through." Children often remember the sequence and say it to themselves as they go through the process. Tying a bow can be difficult for all children and will probably not be accomplished until the child is older. Finding the left shoe from the right is also difficult, and can be made easier by identifying one shoe with, for instance, a piece of tape.

MEALTIMES

The young blind child should now be ready to sit in a regular chair to eat his meals and can remain seated for a much longer period. He should be able to handle a spoon and glass efficiently and should no longer need to pick up food with his fingers. He is now ready to eat from a regular plate rather than a bowl. The use of a small tray will help him to keep his eating utensils in a contained area and to find everything on it with ease. He also can keep all his rejected food on the tray. The right-hand upper corner of the tray is a good place for his glass, so he can find it and put it back easily. Proper eating habits and proper use of utensils will make him more acceptable in a group and will reap rewards when the child is taken to visit friends or to a restaurant. Later on a mat will serve the same purpose as a tray, outlining a circumscribed area.

The food that is placed on a child's plate should be organized so that the meat and vegetables are in the same place each time, or else he should be told where they are (Figure 14-1). Occasionally, the child should be able to serve himself so he remembers that the food comes from a serving bowl. Whatever food is placed on the child's plate should be

Figure 14-1.   A three-year-old girl having mastered a spoon.

identified. Guessing games as to which food is on the plate may be fun, but should be avoided as a matter of routine. The child should no longer have to put his nose into the food to determine what it is. For the blind child, social behavior must be taught, since he cannot learn by imitation.

Once the child is adept at using a spoon, a fork can be introduced. However, it is best to start by having the child pierce a piece of bread. The child should locate the bread and touch it with his fingers; then, with the fork in the other hand, he should pierce the bread. Most blind children are careful enough not to prick their fingers.

A child who is ready to use a fork is also ready to use a

butter knife. To butter a slice of bread, the child will have to reach for the bread, place it on his plate, locate the butter, which should be nearby, hold the knife in one hand, slip some butter onto the knife, and, with his other hand assisting, hold the bread while he spreads the butter. Standing behind the child with your hands on his will help him learn the proper movements. This skill is also best practiced during snack time, when the child has less to distract him.

Using a knife requires much greater skill and the child will not be ready to cut his meat until he is much older. However, at this stage he should know what it means to cut. He can first learn the cutting movement and its results during play with Playdough (Figure 14-2). The child can

Figure 14-2.   Learning to cut with Playdough.

roll the dough into strips, and, with a flat stick, cut the dough into small pieces. After he cuts up a few pieces, he can collect them and put them into a bowl. In that way, he learns that cutting means separating into pieces. Later he can practice cutting soft bread with a dull knife.

Now that the child is older, he is able to participate more in the verbal give and take at the dinner table and should be given the opportunity to do so. Each person at the dinner table should make it a point to talk to the child, remembering to alert him first that he is being addressed, by either calling his name or tapping him gently. Family members can also help the blind child become more aware of what is going on around the dinner table by telling him and describing to him what the others are doing.

Any child, sighted or blind, who can dress, undress, eat with a spoon and fork, butter his bread, pour his own milk, put his clothes away, take care of his toileting needs, and comb his hair is usually very proud of himself. Each time he is successful in acquiring a new skill, he gains more trust in his ability to succeed. The blind child needs to acquire even greater confidence, because future challenges in achieving total independence will require more effort and persistence and far more practice than the sighted child has to exert.

HELPING AROUND THE HOUSE

Sighted children enjoy helping mommy and daddy do chores around the house, and thus learn how beds are made, how tables are set and cleared of soiled dishes, where the dishes go, how laundry is washed, how furniture is dusted, and how simple repairs are made. Most sighted children observe all these activities and, often, if they do not physically take part in them, have some idea of what to do because they have seen others doing them. This is not the case with the blind child. Therefore, as a continuation of what the toddler was taught, we recommend involving the blind child in as many activities of daily living as possible as he becomes capable of doing more, and particularly since this involvement will provide invaluable opportunity for learning. For example, the child can set the table in preparation for the family dinner. He will have to locate the tablecloth or place mats; he must know and remember where they are kept. If place mats are used, he must place each mat in front of each chair, and will have to feel the chair and center the mat accordingly. The next step is to get the plates, with which he will probably need some help. He will have to learn to carry one or more, with care, learning not only how to carry them properly but feeling their weight. At the table, he must now center the plates on the mat. Next he has to get the silverware and to sort the spoons from the forks, which he probably can do well. Now, however, he may have to sort the dinner forks from the dessert forks, a task requiring further discriminating ability. With the forks, spoons, or knives in hand, he will have to learn on which side of the plate the knives, forks, spoons, and napkins need to be placed. If some members of the family get a favorite cup or glass, the child will have to locate that person's seat at the dinner table; he must remember where each member of the family sits, and form a mental image of the family around the table. Because the blind child does not get the visual reward of seeing the finished product, he sometimes resists engaging in such an activity. Therefore, it is important that he hear from family members how well he is doing.

Keeping the blind child involved in daily living activities not only is important so he will learn, but it also keeps him in touch with his environment. Once the child is familiar with the different activities in the home, he will want to take part in them. Parents should assign chores to the blind child just as they would to a sighted child. If the child is treated in the same way as his brothers and sisters, he will be less likely to feel that he is different.

Chapter 15

PRE-READING

PRE-BRAILLE

Reading, another aspect of verbal communication, is a source of information, intellectual stimulation, learning and, last but not least, enjoyment throughout life. The sighted child is exposed to printed words in his picture books, watches his parents and siblings read, and becomes familiar with printed symbols long before he can read. For the blind child, we recommend that parents obtain children's braille books, which also have the printed words, and read them to the child. (These books are available through the American Foundation for the Blind and will be mailed upon request at no cost.)

Blindness does not delay readiness for reading. Like sighted children, some blind children will be ready to read earlier than others, depending on their abilities, experiences, and interests. However, all children must have reached a certain stage of development, physiologically, intellectually and emotionally, to be able to achieve this complex task. While sighted children depend on visual discrimination between the different shapes of the printed letters, the blind child has to learn to discriminate tactually between the configurations of the small braille dots.

The best preparation for this task is the pegboard. It is best to begin with larger pegs and gradually use increasingly smaller ones. Independent of thickness, they should all be short so that the child can feel the top of the peg after he has placed it in the hole. One quarter-inch above the surface of the board is sufficient. If the pegs and board are difficult to purchase, they can be made at home. A set of round holes can be drilled into a board about ten or twelve inches square. The holes must form straight lines, both vertically and horizontally, and be spaced about one-and-a-half inches apart throughout the entire board, adding up to approximately 100 holes (Figure 15-1). The pegs can be cut from round strips of wood (dowels) to fit the holes, and should fit so that they do not tilt in the holes but can be easily removed. These boards and pegs can be made in different sizes, beginning with dowels about a half-inch thick and gradually moving to much thinner ones about one eighth-inch in diameter.

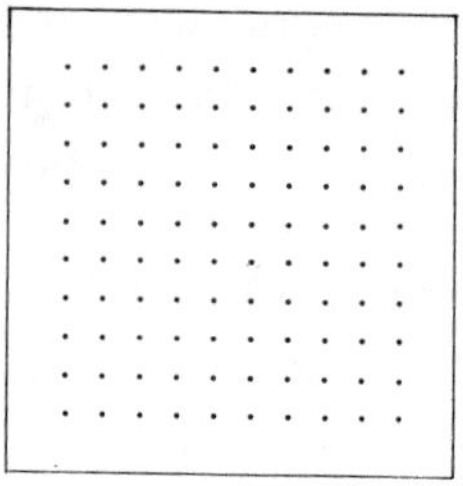

Figure 15-1.

The child should first be encouraged to explore the entire pegboard. With the pegs placed in a box next to the board, the child should feel the pegs and be told that he is to put the pegs in a straight line, either across, upward, or downward, and that he should run his fingers along the straight line of holes, preferably the line nearest the edge first, so that the edge can act as a guide. At the start the board should be covered with cardboard except for the line the child is going to use. Whatever the direction, horizontal or vertical, the child must find the hole (left to right if it is horizontal and top to bottom if it is vertical) and place a peg into it. If the child is right-handed, he should be helped to use the index finger of the left hand as a guide and the right hand to place the peg into the hole. When he is ready for the second peg, the left hand will have to move from the first peg down to the second hole and be held there while he gets another peg to insert. (If he is left-handed the process is reversed.) This continues until the entire row is filled (Figure 15-2). When the child has completed the row, he

Figure 15-2.   Succeeding in placing pegs in vertical straight line.

should run his finger along the row of pegs. When he removes the pegs, he should remove them in the same order he inserted them, thus giving him additional tactual reinforcement of what a straight line is.

There are variations in using pegs. The child may fill two, three, or four rows; he may place the pegs in every other or every third hole, going in either direction; or he may make a "fence" around the pegboard. He may skip one, two, or three rows, etc. He may make a diagonal line. If the child is distracted by the other holes on the board, they should be covered until he has learned to ignore them. It is a great achievement when the child can copy a pattern the adult has made. Blind children are usually able to accomplish this at the time they enter kindergarten. This development parallels the sighted child's ability to copy a circle, a square, and a cross.

TACTILE DISCRIMINATION

After the child has learned to identify objects during his infant and toddler years, he learns that some things are different while others are the same. Since he has already learned to match object to object, he should now be able to match more complex ones from a greater variety. The concept of same and different can now be stressed. Since the child does not see what is so obvious to the sighted child (that is, the difference in appearance) the child may need some training in developing these concepts. Among other things, buttons may be used. Ice cube or candy trays that have individual compartments are excellent for this type of activity. Six different buttons should be put into six spaces, running in a horizontal row. The child will then have to select matching buttons for each cube from another box next to him and place it in the space just below the one he is matching (Figure 15-3). This can be varied from matching very simple buttons to those where discrimination is more difficult.

After the child succeeds with matching, the same trays may be used again, this time for recognizing "different" objects. For this purpose, the parent might assemble several

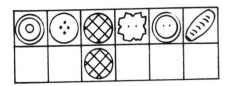

Figure 15-3.

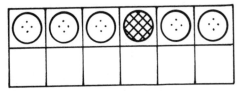

Figure 15-4.

items that are identical and one that is different (Figure 15-4). The child will have to find the one item that is different, and when he does the parent might ask "what makes it different?" This is the kind of training the sighted child receives when he is asked to match pictures or select the one that is different.

In order for the child to learn to perceive fine differences, duplicate pieces of materials might be used, such as wood, metal, sandpaper, plastic, or fabric. For example, if the parent chooses wood, he would need pieces of wood of different textures; if fabric is chosen it would have to be fabric of different textures. These pieces are used most efficiently when cut into three inch squares and pasted on cardboard for the child to feel. In a container next to the child might be the duplicates, which the child will be expected to place under the matching piece (Figure 15-5).

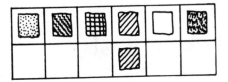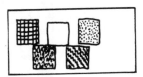

Figure 15-5.

Sorting can also be accomplished with scraps of materials. We have collected all kinds of items, such as empty plastic containers, plastic bottles in different sizes, bottle caps, all types of buttons, empty spools of thread, boxes of all sizes, beads, old keys, cans of different sizes (for example, frozen juice and coffee cans), and all kinds of fabrics. All can be found right in the home or contributed by neighborhood stores. The wallpaper store may supply old sample books which can be used for different textures, the neighborhood lumber yard may supply scraps of wood of different textures and lengths.

When the child learns to sort, the parent can make the game a little more challenging by giving him two criteria. For example, the child can be asked to select all round buttons that are smooth, or all round sticks that are short. These materials can be sorted in a variety of ways—thick and thin, soft and hard, narrow and wide, light and heavy. In arranging these materials, it is best to begin by anchoring down three plastic containers grouped together, and either gluing them to a piece of cardboard or placing them in a box that fits them well enough so that they don't move and distract the child. The size of the containers will depend on the size of the material to be sorted. The center container should have the assorted materials the child is going to separate. For example, if the goal is to teach rough and smooth, and buttons are being used, the rough and smooth buttons should be in the middle container. The child should feel all three containers and be asked to place all the rough buttons in the container on the right and all the smooth buttons in the container on the left (Figure 15-6). Children

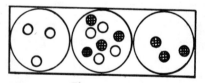

Figure 15-6.

usually love this activity; sometimes the noise the items produce as they hit the containers adds to the attraction for the blind child. This can be a great deal of fun as well as an educational experience.

The sorting materials we have just described can be found in the home or neighborhood stores and are simple to collect. However, when the child is ready for more advanced grouping of objects into "families" or categories, such as fruit, vegetables, furniture, kitchen utensils, or objects for transportation, they become somewhat more difficult to collect. However, a good many may be found in the dime store. When the sighted child is ready to sort in this manner, he can do so by using picture representations. The blind child needs objects.

After the parents have collected several objects belonging to each "family," the child should separate them, using the technique used previously—placing the objects into the designated containers, for example all furniture in one container and all kitchen utensils in another.

Progressing further, the child can separate these items using other criteria, dividing furniture, for example, into bedroom, living room, and dining room. Kitchen utensils can be separated into those used for eating and those used for cooking. Other objects might be sorted into those that are edible and those that are not. Vehicles can be separated into cars, trucks, and police cars.

Understanding sequence is the basis for many functions. As the toddler learned the sequence of graded cups, the young child can now move on to more complex tasks. Pieces of wood or fabric may now be arranged according to different thickness, width, texture, length, size, etc. For example, if the child is to grade lengths of wood, the task could be presented by gluing about eight pieces of varying lengths of wood on a cardboard, in a sequence beginning with either the shortest or the longest. They can be placed either horizontally or vertically on the cardboard.

There should be sufficient room left on the board for the child to reproduce the identical sequence with another set, either below or next to the one pasted on the board. After the child feels the different lengths that are on the board, he can be given the unattached set and asked to place the components in the identical order (Figure 15-7). After he has learned to reproduce the order, he can then try to repeat it from memory.

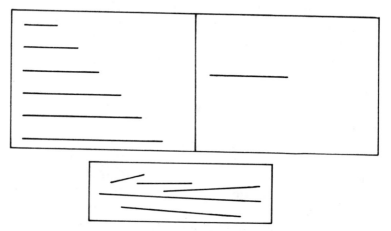

Figure 15-7.

The sighted child is exposed to patterns occurring in the environment—patterns of color, texture, etc. The blind child who cannot see patterns has to be helped to experience them by touch. Patterns can also be arranged by pasting them on cardboard, using the same materials as those employed for sequencing. For example, if fabric is used, alternating pieces of rough and smooth, etc., repeated perhaps five times, can be pasted on the board. Again sufficient space must be left on the board for the child to reproduce the pattern with an identical unattached set. These patterns can be designed in many ways, such as two rough and one smooth, or one smooth and three rough, etc. If necessary, additional pieces may be added, up to about twelve or fourteen. After the child has learned to repeat patterns, he should be encouraged to create some of his own.

Once the child has explored the various materials on the board, he should be helped to find objects made of similar materials in the home. He could go on a hunt to find everything made of metal, glass, wood, fabric, plastic, and so forth.

Children need many experiences in matching, sorting, categorizing, sequencing, and patterning. The greater the range of materials used, the greater his experience and his ability to classify and learn the different characteristics of each object. We have only mentioned a few as a start. Parents are creative and will soon follow with their own ideas.

The sighted child first learns to understand relationships visually. He sees the fireman ride the engine, the postman bring the mail, etc. When the sighted child gets older, he can demonstrate this by combining a picture of a fireman with an engine, a letter with a postman, and so on. In order for the blind child to make the appropriate association, he must first know the fireman, by touching and talking to him, by exploring the engine, etc. The objects that were used previously can now be used to teach these relationships. The parent can select a few items, such as the baby doll and the baby bottle, or the bathtub and the soap. The parent can show and describe to the child how these objects are related and later have the child demonstrate his understanding.

COUNTING

Most children learn to count by rote. However, the sighted child sees objects in one, two, or larger groups and soon will not only count them correctly, but will also develop the concept of oneness, twoness, etc. The blind child will have to count actual objects by touching each one to be able to learn those concepts. Fortunately, there are many opportunities in the course of a day to make counting fun. Counting his fingers is the simplest and most natural way for the child to start.

Sighted young children observe that when a cup full of beans is poured into a smaller cup, it will spill over, or if a full cup of water is poured into a pint container, it will not fill it. Although they do not understand the principle involved, having observed it will later enable them to comprehend the reason. The blind child misses this observation and must be helped to experience it by feeling the different levels.

Thermic (temperature) and baric (weight) sensitivity can be developed by the same kind of matching and sequencing that is done tactually and auditorily. The materials needed for this can also be found in the home— eight-ounce plastic bottles for instance, or small metal containers. The parent might fill three or four of these with water of extreme temperatures such as hot and very cold. Two sets of these will be needed so the child can match pairs as he did with other materials to develop the tactile sense.

For sequencing, the parent will need to arrange the containers in the proper order and add a few more; for example, hot, slightly warmer than tepid, tepid, cooler, cold, and ice cold. After the child feels each one, the parent can rearrange them and ask the child to put them in the proper sequence either beginning with hot or ice cold.

A similar arrangement can be made with the same containers using materials to fill them that will demonstrate weights instead of different temperatures. Use small pieces of metal, rocks, stones, or any small object that will fit into the containers. Again, the parent will need two matching sets of three or four different weights of gross differences, which the child can match using the same technique he did with the temperature. After the child has learned to match the weights, the parent may arrange a sequence of very light,

light, medium, heavy, heavier, and heaviest containers. Many gradations can be made until the child can perceive very fine differences.

The olfactory sense (smell) must also be developed; similar containers can be used, inserting small amounts of various condiments into each container—cinnamon, cloves, bay leaves, nutmeg, etc. As before, using two matching sets of four different fragrances is best for the beginner. A number of items can be added since there are many things in the home the child will enjoy smelling and matching: for example, face powder, lipstick, perfume, dusting powder. Other aromas—candy, tea, coffee, mint, as well as fruits of all kinds—might be used. Sequencing scents or fragrances presents a problem and may be difficult because degrees of intensity may vary with quantity.

It is not sufficient, however, to receive sensations. What we perceive through our senses has to be processed to lead to conceptualizations and generalizations and eventually to abstractions. As the child develops he recognizes character- istics and moves from grouping identical to somewhat different objects, from single to groups of objects with common attributes, and then to collective categories. The young blind child has more difficulty in reaching these developmental stages, since his identifying landmarks are fewer, less informative, and more elusive. To illustrate: The blind young child knows his own hat. He then touches his father's hat, and despite the different feeling of texture, shape, and size, learns that it, too, is a hat. When he later encounters his mother's hat, the common quality remains their purpose—all three are worn on the head to protect and give warmth. To give another example: A child is told that he is touching glass, and it is smooth. Another time he might touch glass and it is not smooth, but it is still glass. The child needs to learn that objects have different attributes; for example, that glass may have many shapes, textures, and sizes. In sighted children this presents little difficulty. The blind child has to be provided with many varied experiences to enable him to transfer, generalize, and integrate what he has experienced and learned.

How well blind children can do this was illustrated when one of our teachers* took her group of five- and six-year-old visually-impaired children to the circus. It is an excellent example of how a totally blind five-year-old was able to utilize previous learning, and shows that although lack of vision limits the experience, by no means does it prevent the blind child from enjoying it and being enriched by it.

> During the first act, the child listened for cues. He was given a verbal description of all activities taking place in the ring, described as the center stage, a word familiar to the child from school. He questioned the teacher each time the sounds changed by asking, "And now what's going on, what are they doing?" After being told that the snapping sound in the first act was that of a trainer's whip hitting the floor to make the lions move, he later asked if the elephant trainer was making the elephants move, too, after hearing the same whip sound during this later act. He later laughed loudly when the teacher described the acrobats' act. After listening to the lion cages being emptied as the lions ran through the interlocking cages into the ring, he wanted to know whether the clinking sounds came from a lock. At the end of the act, he remarked that the lions were going back when he heard them running through again.

AUDITORY DISCRIMINATION

Listening to and discriminating between sounds begins in infancy when the baby hears and soon recognizes his parents' voices, and reacts to sounds and noises, turning toward their source. During infancy and the toddler stage, he

---

*Florence Hirschberg

has learned to interpret the meaning of sounds—the spoon clicking against the cup announcing food, the mother's footsteps indicating her approach. The child has gradually learned the meaning of many sounds and voices, loving, praising or scolding; some gentle and some more emphatic. Eventually, he understands that words have various specific meanings and that they can be used to get what one wants or reject what one does not want. For the sighted child, words are illustrated by the objects or movements that accompany them. The blind child has to listen more carefully, more often, and try harder to remember what he has heard. For the blind child hearing will become a finely tuned instrument registering the slightest changes. Therefore, sound discrimination is indispensable and has to be learned.

In the same manner that a child learns to match objects he can now learn to match sounds. Material used for this purpose can be made easily at home. We use empty metal film containers that are shaped like cylinders, but any small metal container found in the home may be used. A small amount of noise-producing materials can be put into each container: salt, marbles, rice, or paper clips. It is best to begin with eight containers, two each producing the same sound, four matching sets in all. The sounds should be very different at first; for example, the very soft sound of salt, compared with the louder sound made by marbles or small rocks. The sound of a few nails or paper clips might be added later. Sometimes the size and quantity of the materials used and the type of container affect the sound, and an effort should be made to eliminate these differences.

After the quality of the sound is established, the parent can give the child a set of four different-sounding cylinders, which the child can shake and listen to and then place on the table. The parent selects one sound from the other set and asks the child to find one like it. When the child finds its mate, he sets them both aside. The parent continues with this until the child has matched all four sets. Additional cylinders may be added as the child becomes more proficient. Gradually, the differences in sound can be reduced until they are very slight. It is important to keep the room quiet during these activities to avoid interference and distraction.

The next step is to give the child several identical sound-producing containers and one that is different, and ask him to find the different one. Again, when teaching same and different it is best to begin with gross differences, and move gradually to finer distinctions.

Just as the child learned to sequence tactually, he will learn to sequence pitch and loudness auditorily. Therefore, a set of sound-making cylinders should be arranged in sequence ranging from the softest to the loudest sounds. At first, the parents will have to arrange them, but later the child should be expected to set up the correct sequence by himself.

Patterns of sound and rhythm can also be arranged, for example two soft and two loud. A variety of sound patterns can be made, encouraging the child to create his own. Rhythmic sound patterns can also be created by beating a drum, tapping the floor with the foot or a stick, hand clapping, etc., and they can be varied in many ways. Here, too, softness and loudness can be used by alternating two soft, one loud, two loud and one soft sound, etc. Or else speed might be introduced by using fast and slow rhythms. The child will learn to imitate these patterns if he is exposed to them gradually.

The role hearing and touch play in the life of the blind child and adult is evident. Less noticeable is the importance of sensitivity to temperature and weight as sources of information. The early awareness and utilization of these should, therefore, be part of a blind child's education. The young blind child will soon learn that the warm touch of the windowsill means the sun is shining or that the light weight of the cup indicates that it is empty.

Chapter 16

LEARNING THROUGH PLAY

The importance of play and the amount of learning that takes place through play have been discussed previously. We cannot stress enough that unless the blind child is made aware of all the activities he can engage in and enjoy, he is not likely to become involved. The sighted child sees how family members busy themselves and sometimes he will take part in what the others are doing; the blind child has to be introduced to these activities (Figure 16-1).

As an accepted member of the family, the young blind child is well able and should be given the opportunity to participate in holiday preparations and activities. Since he cannot receive the visual impressions, actually taking part will enable him to experience the mood of the rituals, the joy of sharing, making decorations, and tasting special foods.

Another experience the child should not be deprived of is caring for living things, such as plants and animals. Unless the child's attention is drawn to these, he will have little interest in them. When planting, it is a good idea to

Figure 16-1.   Water play.

involve the child by purchasing the seeds with him and have him put them into the soil, whether it be in a pot or the garden (Figure 16-2). As the child waters the seeds, he should feel the soil for moisture and for sprouts from time to time and "watch" the process of growth. Our children planted tomato seeds in window boxes on their play roof and later were delighted to pick tomatoes, which they ate as part of their lunch. The children also planted flowers, which they watered and "watched" grow.

Just as many sighted children enjoy pets and caring for them, so do blind children. They can feed the animals, empty the can of dog or cat food into the animal's dish, give it water, and take on the same responsibilities as their sighted peers.

Woodworking is another activity blind children can learn to do safely and enjoyably. A parent must, however, be able to judge when the child is ready for it. If he is adept at using small pegs, stringing small beads, or opening and

Figure 16-2.   Planting.

closing bottles or jars, he should be ready to engage in
woodwork. Not all sighted or blind children are interested in
this craft.

Before the child begins a woodworking project, he will
need to know how to hammer a nail into wood. Learning to
do so may take a little practice. Experience has shown us that
very rarely will a blind child who has been taught to use a

hammer and nails bang his fingers, an incident that is not uncommon in sighted children. Woodworking enhances the child's ability to grasp the shape and form of many objects. Whether he is making a car, a table, a wagon, or a house, he will produce the total form of these objects. It will help to show him a finished product beforehand so he has some idea of what it might look like.

Most young sighted children love to cut and paste. Using scissors properly takes quite a bit of practice. The young blind child will have to be shown how to hold the paper in one hand and the scissors in the other. Since he is still too young for precise cutting, he can cut paper for collages, which can be in any shape or form. Before pasting, the child should be shown the boundaries of the paper he is using and where the paste and paper are placed. He should also be given some idea of the many ways the paper can be arranged: close together, spread out, to one side, etc. He can then make his own patterns. Taking the time to show the child all the materials and where they are on the table is important in order to avoid distractions.

Many things can be used for collages—small pieces of fabric, old buttons, artificial flowers, pieces of cotton, pebbles, yarn, cork, styrofoam, or other odds and ends found in the home. The pleasure of creating something, particularly something the child can feel, and sharing of the finished product with his family are as important to blind as they are to sighted children.

Throughout his life, the blind child will have to depend on memory. When he is getting dressed, he will have to remember the combination of clothes and the various identifications on the clothes. When traveling, he will have to remember the number of stops, in their proper sequence, on the train or subway. When walking he may need to remember which intersections to cross, when to make turns, etc. Acquiring a good memory is vital to the blind child and can be furthered through games. For example, place three objects on the table in front of the child and have him feel them. After they are removed, he should recall what they were. If he succeeds, a few more items can be added. After he accomplishes that, he might be asked to remember the order in which he touched them. Later, one item can be removed and the child asked whether he knows which one is missing.

Simple board games played with other children can also be enjoyed by the blind child, as long as he can understand and follow simple directions and the rules of the game, as well as some of the competitive aspects of them. Many board games can be adapted very easily for blind children by adding texture to pieces so the child can recognize them. Checkers can be adapted by pasting a different texture on either the black or red squares on the board, and the corresponding texture on the checkers themselves. Some domino sets are available with raised or indented dots, which the blind child can feel and count.

Blind children enjoy block building as do their sighted peers. Of course, the blind child will have to be introduced to blocks and given some idea of the many possibilities for their use. Showing the child how to build a house, a road, a tunnel, a bridge, or a street is an excellent way to teach him how roads curve, or how cars go through tunnels, or over bridges, etc. With a little assistance and by demonstrating several finished models, the child will soon be able to build independently.

Cooking is another activity that fosters learning. In the kitchen the blind child learns what foods are like before they are prepared, which are soft, hard, cold, hot, etc. He will experience that one whole can be cut into halves, quarters, etc. He will learn how much is in a cupful, a spoonful, and how some foods are peeled. He can learn much just from pouring, mixing, beating, breaking eggs, and the many processes necessary for preparing a meal. If the child does not actively participate in these activities he may think all cookies come from boxes, or eggs come prepared as an omelet, or that spaghetti is always soft (Figure 16-3). Buying, preparing, cooking, setting a table, serving, and cleaning up afterwards can be a very rich experience for the child and an excellent opportunity for the parents to interact with him.

Figure 16-3.   Children popping corn.

The sighted child also learns from and enjoys these experiences, but for the blind child this kind of involvement is an absolute necessity, because it serves as a training ground for indispensible special skills the sighted child does not have to depend on.

When the child is taken to the market, he should be allowed to touch some of the shelves—lifted up to them if necessary—and shown how high they are and how the items are grouped into canned foods, frozen foods, dairy foods, etc. At the fruit and vegetable section, he can be shown which produce are fruits and which are vegetables. Show him how the plastic bags in the fruit and vegetable departments are dispensed on a roller. Let him pull a bag off the roll and help put the items in the bag. (Pointing out the plastic bags and other seemingly insignificant actions are so easily overlooked, but the child has no idea of where the bags come from unless he is shown.) Have the child help put the groceries into the cart. At the check-out counter, let him help remove them and place them on the counter. Explain to him what the cashier is doing. If the child is not actively involved, he remains in a world of meaningless sound, and although you may tell him that the clicking sound is the cash register, he will have no idea of its shape or whether it is suspended from the ceiling or held in someone's hands.

There will be occasions when parents will hesitate to allow a child to tactually explore objects, particularly in a store, because they fear it may be offensive. In such instances, we recommend that parents explain the reason to the store owner or manager and reassure him that they will supervise the child at all times. This may be difficult for some parents to do, but it will avoid discomfort or embarrassment if done before the child actually begins touching objects. The blind child who is permitted to explore a store gets as much pleasure as the sighted child does from looking. When a parent takes the child to stores where there are many counters or shelves stacked with items, such as a supermarket or a department store, it is best to allow him to explore only a few counters or shelves at a time so he is not overwhelmed or overstimulated.

Imagination is the manifestation of an active mind. In the young child it finds expression in the form of play and stimulates intellectual development and creativity. Like sighted children, blind children will engage in make believe activities. However, the meaning of pretending will have to be explained to the blind child since he cannot see others pantomiming or imitating. It is interesting to observe how quickly the child learns to use pantomime once the idea of make believe is understood. Just as sighted children pretend they are doctors, mommies, daddies, postmen, ice cream vendors, conductors, bus drivers, etc., so do blind children, and with the same joy as their sighted friends.

We have stressed the importance of outings for the blind child from the time he is a baby. They are extremely important to the child's development in helping him gain knowledge of his world. Although the child is blind the parents need not hesitate to take him to the zoo, the museum, "to watch" the circus, or a children's show, or to any other place children enjoy. The child should have enough language by this age to understand verbal descriptions and will derive much pleasure from the trip. Including the child on these excursions is important for another reason, too. Although he cannot see the animals in the zoo, the child does gain some information and a much better idea of what a zoo or a circus is like and will be better able to understand when he hears others talk about it. Otherwise, the child may say "a zoo is where animals are" but will not have the slightest notion of what the words mean.

When a blind child feels an object, he depends on his sense of touch. However, like sighted individuals who miss visually obvious things in their environment, so may a blind person "not see something with his hands." We called the parents' attention to this earlier, but now that the child is older, it is important to observe once again whether he is using his hands purposefully and efficiently because he is now ready to perceive more. The blind child, like his sighted peers, must learn to be a better observer. The parents should look at how the child moves his hands when he is "looking" at an object. Are his hands moving too fast? Is he palming the object and not using the fingertips which are more sensitive? One indication of the inefficient use of hands is too quick a movement, such as all over a table, grabbing at everything they come in contact with but "seeing" little. If the child has difficulty controlling his hands it is best to ask him to put his hands in his lap until the object is presented to him. If the child's hands still move too fast, it is best to gently hold his hands and show him how to move them slowly over the object, using his fingertips.

When the baby begins to explore, he will not perceive all the details of an object, just as the sighted child does not see all the details at first. The sighted child looking at picture books will perceive more details in a picture every time he looks at it. The blind child's hands will function in a similar manner. Some children's hands need little training, just as some sighted children will notice more at once than others. The child needs to be given the opportunity of "seeing" objects several times, with more and more details pointed out to him on each occasion. The child who has the proper training will spontaneously ask "what's this?" as he discovers a new detail.

We have observed blind children who dislike touching certain objects, perhaps because they are soft, wet, or rough. This is always of some concern, because it limits the use of an all-important sense and cuts off a vital source of information. In such instances, rather than have the child touch the object with his hands, have him first touch the object with his feet. Except for wet or hot articles, the child will generally be willing to touch almost anything with his feet. Start gently and slowly by placing the object on the soles of the child's feet; gradually move the object up to his leg, then up toward his arms, neck, and face. It may take a month or more of doing this, once a day for a few minutes each time, before he is ready to touch with his hands. Even then one should proceed slowly; just let him touch an object for a fleeting moment at first, and gradually increase the time with each subsequent attempt.

A wet substance such as finger paint, so commonly used in schools, are sometimes a bit difficult for the child to accept. If the parents want to use it, it is best to give the child a small piece of sponge about two inches square and have him move the paint around with the sponge rather than with his fingers. Some of the paint is bound to touch the child's fingers, and he will gradually become accustomed to the feel of the finger paint.

Most children have a desire to "make things." Their natural creative impulse finds many ways of expression, stimulated by what they see in their small world. Clay or similar material serves in imitating forms and creating new ones, in kneading, shaping, and reshaping.

Although these activities involve the sense of touch in the sighted as well as the blind child, the latter, unable to see clay and what others do with it, will have to be introduced to it cautiously. If he is reluctant to touch this strange material, start with plasticine or Playdough instead, since they are not as wet or sticky. If problems persist, the parent can shape and mold the clay. As they work with it, the child can place his hands on the parent's hands. If this activity is done frequently, perhaps once a week, the child will gradually get used to it. After the child becomes accustomed to using clay, it will prove to be an excellent medium to practice making circles and straight and curved lines, particularly because its indentations can easily be felt by the child.

Another good medium to start off with is water and Ivory Snow or Flakes. Because the child is familiar with soap, he is apt to accept it. The parent may put a small amount of flakes into a cupful of water, which the child can play with. Gradually more soap can be added until it forms a paste and becomes pliable. It is important to add the soap very gradually. The child can then spread this paste on paper, where it will eventually harden into a "painting" that he can feel. A small amount of fingerpaint can be added for color.

Chapter 17

FIRST AWARENESS OF BLINDNESS

During the first few years of life, blind children are unaware of their condition. If born blind, they assume that everyone else experiences the world in the same way they do. It is not unusual for a young blind child to show his mother something for her to put her hands on, a demonstration that he assumes that she, too, sees with her hands. Or, as one blind adult remembered, he assumed when he was a child that others who saw objects he could not see had much longer arms. Becoming aware of being blind is a developmental process that depends on age. Although we have had children at the Child Development Center sense their difference as early as three years of age, they are the exception. Generally, the child begins to ask questions when he is about five. Although blind children may use the term "blind and blindness" and may appear to understand it, they usually do not. It may take them months or years to fully comprehend what being blind means.

Their first awareness that they are different occurs quite

naturally, usually when others are commenting on something the blind child cannot see, such as a picture, or possibly a bird, which the child can only hear. If the blind child asks to see the picture or feel the bird he begins to question why he is told he cannot see it. Another quite common cause for beginning awareness is when the child asks the parent to look at something he made. If the adult does not get close and feel it with his hands, the child may get upset, refusing to believe that it can be seen from across the room. Sometimes, the beginning awareness comes very subtly. In one instance, a child came into the playground and could not understand how his favorite bike could be recognized and taken so quickly by his partially sighted friend. Another blind child might question how an adult, upon entering a room, can recognize all the children when the children do not greet her. These types of incidents occur quite frequently during the course of a day at home and at school. Since the realization that they are blind is generally very gradual, it may seem as though children understand, yet will respond in a manner that makes it doubtful. For example, one bright five year old, who appeared to know he was blind, still could not understand how his teacher knew he had a new haircut without touching his head. This confusion is common in young blind children, and shows their struggle and efforts to understand.

When the children realize they are blind and that they are unable to do certain things their sighted peers can, they may become either depressed or angry. Although this is painful to both parents and the child, it is a stage the child must go through to learn to deal with his blindness. Parents can help the blind child through this difficult period by verbalizing the child's feelings and the parents' understanding and acceptance of them. Even if the child is not able to express the reason for his anger or depression, the parent should try to talk about the child's feelings with him. Because the child cannot see the facial expressions on his parents' faces, he needs to be told that they truly understand his feelings and the difficult time he is going through. For example, a parent might say "You are angry because you would like to see the picture that everyone else is talking about," or "You are feeling quite unhappy because you think you can't do what Johnny is doing." The verbalization of the child's feelings should relate directly to the activity that the child is particularly upset about. It should not refer to a past or future event.

Some children express their frustration and feeling of anger by insisting that they want to see or that they will be able to see when they grow up. Although they may persist several times, parents should try not to become upset and recognize that it is another way for their child to question why he is blind and express his frustration.

Often, after a child realizes and begins to deal with the fact that he is different from other children, he begins to question why. The question may indeed be phrased, "Why am I blind?" This question may also be asked by siblings or other children. Some parents choose to answer these questions in religious terms. Others may choose to give the child a direct answer by telling him that he was born blind just as other people are born unable to hear or unable to walk. Whatever the answer, the parent must reassure the child of all the things he *can* do, by listing his accomplishments and stressing the fact that he is loved by his family and friends.

The blind child may become more aware of the difference between himself and his sighted peers and begin to question why he is blind when he cannot be left on his own for safety reasons. He wonders why his sighted peers are far more independent, for example, in an outdoor park, on the street, or at a lake or swimming pool. The blind child, who may consider himself quite independent and capable of caring for himself, may resent having to be supervised and not being allowed to go out on his own. However, the parents should explain to him that, indeed, they are not allowing him to do any of these activities on his own because they must take safety measures. The situation may be somewhat difficult and painful for the parents and the child. However, the child needs to feel that his parents care for him and will protect him from harm. The parents should make certain that the limitations they impose are necessary and the danger real, and allow him independence when there is no danger. In addition to realizing that there are places that are unsafe for him and where he will need supervision, the blind child also needs to learn that there are situations in which he needs to ask for help from a sighted person and that it is all right for him to do so. In his attempt to become independent, the blind child sometimes resists asking for help. However, part of their realization that they are blind and their acceptance and ability to cope with their impairment is accepting that in some situations they cannot function unless a sighted person assists them. Parents must be sensitive to this need and help the child understand it. In cases in which the blind child does not need help, he should learn to say, "No, thank you." This is a very difficult issue for most parents to deal with. The frustration of being blind may reoccur. Parents will always feel pain as situations arise and stir these feelings, but most parents learn to cope with them. Most try their very best to help the child understand what it means to be blind and how to accept it. How the parent handles this will determine how the child views himself. If he knows he is cared for and his feelings are understood and accepted, his impairment will be easier for him to bear. However, the parent must also expect the child to function within his ability and with a goal toward total independence. If the child is expected to perform, he will view himself as capable, and his attitude toward his blindness will be realistic.

As we have tried to demonstrate throughout, the blind child can grow and develop as the sighted child does, although he needs intervention. Parents often ask whether the blind child can grow up to be independent and productive, and are sometimes surprised when they hear that their child can go on to higher education, if he has the necessary intellectual capacity and emotional balance. As we have stated, blindness need not retard the development of a child. Blind children's potential varies just as it does for sighted children, and ranges from the intellectually gifted to the slow learner. Provision should be made for the blind child to obtain the type of education that best meets his abilities.

A word of caution to parents of blind children: Do not lose perspective of the child's ability and readiness. Often, in the parents' desire to move the child from one step to another at a faster rate, the parent may put undue pressure on him. The child must take each step at his own pace. The rate of development varies with each child, as it does with sighted children. If a parent senses considerable lags in development, problems other than blindness should be explored.

Chapter 18

MULTIPLE IMPAIRMENTS

Children with visual impairments are first and foremost children. They are, therefore, liable to show the same developmental dysfunctions and disorders that can be found in any group of children. Language and learning disabilities, behavioral and emotional disturbances, or retardation lie within the range of possibility. The child who has more than one dysfunction, moreover, is caught in a special dilemma since each dysfunction is likely to compound the adverse effect of the other.

It is tempting and not at all uncommon to attribute deviations in development or functions to the lack of vision. This puts the child in further jeopardy since it postpones or prevents early recognition of the cause of the problem and the necessary intervention at a time when it might be most effective, i.e., the early years of the child's development.

To prevent this from happening, we have listed below some of the symptoms that may be indicative of problems not related to blindness. While *none* of the following symptoms are significant when observed in isolated instances, when they are present most of the time and for a prolonged period of time, or when more than one symptom is observed and persists, the parents might do well to seek professional advice.

The infant

Failure to smile back when talked to.

Excessive irritability.

Inability to adjust to changes in position, environment, or feeding.

Failure to respond and turn to sound or touch.

Failure to grasp. Failure to remove diaper from face.

Failure to roll over, sit up, pull to standing position, or walk at expected age.

Failure to imitate simple activities, such as ringing a bell, pulling a toy to activate it.

Absence of vocalizing, babbling, imitating sounds.

Excessive rocking.

Intolerance of cuddling or expressions of affection.

The toddler

Excessive rocking.

Excessive twirling (to the exclusion of most other activities).

Excessive spinning of movable parts of toys and objects.

Failure to crawl or walk at the end of the toddler stage.

No attempts at locomotion.

No attempts at communication.

Failure to respond to or turn to source of sound.

Failure to respond to spoken language.

Absence of words.

Lack of interest in and failure to interact with environment.

Inability to imitate.

The young child

Failure to crawl, walk, or use any kind of locomotion.

Inability to recognize what should be familiar objects or to use them.

Inability to recognize members of the family by voice.

Lack of speech.

Inability to understand spoken language.

Inconsistent or no response to sounds.

Persistent echolalia (repetition of what is said without comprehension).

Short attention span (inability to remain seated for about thirty minutes while engaged in an activity).

As the child increases in age, the symptoms listed above take on greater significance. At the same time, it must be remembered that young children in the process of developing have a tendency to regress to earlier stages for short periods. This may occur when new skills are being developed, causing additional strain and frustration, or when emotional stress interferes with the child's ability to cope. These interludes are part of normal development and are not under consideration here.

LETTER TO A MOTHER

Dear Mother:

As you were reading these pages, you may have been wondering why we so persistently addressed ourselves to the parent and not to the mother. We did this because we wanted to stress the partnership of parents in the pains and joys of bringing up a blind child—or any child. We want to assure you that at the same time we were fully aware of the fact that you, as a mother, carry the heavier burden both emotionally and physically.

If, nevertheless, we ask you to do even more for your blind child, it is because we share your concern for your child and want you to benefit from the experience and success of other mothers and their blind children.

We want to convey to you the urgency of intervention to prevent lack of vision from interfering with the stimulation and experience necessary for the normal development of your child. By investing the additional thought, energy, and time, you will have laid the foundation for a satisfying, fulfilled life for the entire future of your child. We urge you to try, and hope that you may find our suggestions helpful and a source of joy for both you and your child.

Shulamith Kastein
Isabelle Spaulding
Battia Scharf

SUGGESTED READINGS

Brazelton, T. B. Infants and Mothers. In *Differences in development.* New York: Dell, 1969.

Brazelton, T. B. *Toddlers and parents.* New York: Delacorte, 1974.

Cratty, J. *Movement and spatial awareness in blind children and youth.* Springfield, Illinois: Charles C. Thomas, 1971.

Cronin, J. M. Preschool learning activities for the visually impaired child. In *A guide for parents,* State Board of Education, Illinois Office of Education.

Davidson, I., Fletcher, J., Howard, M., Joech, I., Santin, S., Simmons, J. N., & Weaver, D. *Handbook for parents of preschool blind children.* Toronto: Ontario Institute for Studies in Education, 1976.

Drouillard, R. & Raynor, S. *Move it: A guide for helping visually impaired children grow.* Ingham Intermediate School District, Michigan, 1977.

Faye, E. E. *The low vision patient.* New York: Grune and Stratton, 1970.

Fraiberg, S. *The magic years.* New York: Scribners, 1959.

Fraiberg, S. *Insights from the blind.* New York: Basic Books, 1977.

Gershe, L. *Butterflies are free.* New York: Random House, 1970.

Jan, J., Freeman, R., & Scott, E. *Visual impairment in children and adolescents.* New York: Grune and Stratton, 1977.

Kastein, S. & Trace, B. *The birth of language.* Springfield, Illinois: Charles C. Thomas, 1966.

Levy, J. *The baby exercise book.* New York: Pantheon Books, 1973.

Raynor, S. & Drouillard, R. *Get and wiggle on.* Ingham, Michigan: Ingham Intermediate School District, 1975.

Scott, E., Jan, J. & Freeman, J. *Can't your child see.* Baltimore: University Park Press, 1977.

Sullivan, T. *If you could see what I could hear.* New York: Harper and Row, 1975.

RESOURCE INFORMATION

Directory of Agencies Serving the Visually Handicapped in the United States, Twentieth Edition. New York: American Foundation for the Blind, 1978.

Closer Look
Bureau of Education for the Handicapped
Box 1492
Washington, D.C. 20013

INDEX

Adhesive tape use, 154–155
American Foundation for the
    Blind, 165
Anger
    awareness of blindness and,
        190–191
    displacement by parents
        onto healthy child, 20
Arm and shoulder exercises,
    39
Auditory discrimination, in
    young children, 176–178
Auditory signals. *See* Sound
Auditory stimulation
    and mobiles, 76
    and radios and record
        players, 66, 77, 135

Ball playing, 132–133
Barefoot play, 134

Baths, 126–127
Beads, stringing, 131
Bells, on targets, 133. *See
    also* Doorbells; Mobiles
Blindfolding, and selection of
    toys, 83–84
Blindisms and mannerisms,
    86–87
Blindness
    acceptance of limitations
        of, 19–20
    child's reactions to, 189–
        193
    potential and, 21–22,
        192–193
    and recognition of other
        impairments, 194–196
Block play, 131–132, 183
    in playground, 146
Board games, 183
Body concept, 96

Body contact, 62–63
    games for, 78–79
    in toddler stage, 118–119
Body parts, naming of, 79, 96
Boots, putting on, 158–159
Bottle feeding, sound during,
    52–53
Bouncing, in walker, 44
Braille. *See* Pre-braille
    training
Bristle blocks, 130–131
Brushing teeth, 156–157
"Busy boxes," 78
Butter knife, 161–162
Buttoning, 159–160

Child Development Center,
    21, 189
Circus visits, 176, 186
Clay, 188
Climbing, 50
Collages, 182
Color coordination, 158
Cooking, 183–184
Community relations, of
    parents of blind child,
    15
Compliments, verbal, 124
Counting, 173–176
Crawling and creeping, 46–48
Creeping. *See* Crawling and
    creeping
Cruising, in infancy, 47–48
Cup or glass
    drinking from, 56–57
    graded, 130
    placing back on table,
    ˙112–113
    throwing, 57
Cutting with knife, 161–162

Cutting and pasting, 182

Depth perception, 93
Developmental gap, between
    blind and sighted
    children, 80–81
Depression, and awareness of
    blindness, 190–191
Distance, judgement of, 32
Dolls, in orientation learning,
    147–148
Door(s)
    to house, chime over, 134
    opening and closing, 79–80,
    82–83, 93
    opening with key, 154
Doorbell ringing, 68
Dressing and undressing
    preparation in infancy, 60
    and selection of clothing,
    158, 159
    in toddler stage, 122–126
    and young children,
    157–160
Drinking
    from cup, 56–57
    placing glass or cup back
    on table, 112–113

Eating, speech readiness and,
    35–36. *See also*
    Infant feeding; Finger
    foods; Mealtime
Educational toys, 81–82
Emotional development
    language development and,
    143
    in toddler stage, 120–122
Emotions

[Emotions]
and awareness of blindness,
190–191
conveying with voice, 33
Environment
awareness in infancy of,
31–34
exploration of, 70–71
familiarity with, walking
and, 93–94
See also Mobility
Exercises, 38–39, 145
Experiences
language learning and, 35
unpleasant or painful,
preparation for, 122
Eye contact, substitutes for,
67–68, 103–104
Eyes, pressing with fingers,
86, 87

Family
and birth of blind child,
15–17
income, 15
at mealtime, 55–56, 111–
112, 113, 164
names of members of,
102–103
recognition of members
of, 33
Fantasy, separation from
reality, 105. *See also*
Imagination
Fear
of sitting down from
standing position, 46
of swimming, 98
of touching new toy,
107–108
Feeding: stimulation during,

37–38. *See also* Food;
Infant feeding; Mealtime
Feet, touching things with,
49, 187
Fine motor development
in infancy, 51
in toddler stage, 99–100
in young children, 154–155
Finger food, 57–58, 112
Finger paints, 187–188
Floors, bare, 49
Food
and chewing as exercise for
fine motor development,
51
organization on plate, 161
rejected, 58
See also Finger food,
Infant feeding; Mealtime
Food market, trips to,
184–185
Footsteps, recognition of,
33, 38
Fork use, 161–162
Form box, homemade, 132
Furniture. *See* Household
furnishings

Gagging, on solid foods,
54–55
Games
during crawling or walking,
67
for detection of obstacles,
152–153
to enhance listening skills,
101–102
for fine motor coordina-
tion, 154–155
to improve walking, 50
for left-right differentiation,
149

[Games]
for memory improvement,
182–183
for sound matching,
177–178
teaching space and location
concepts, 145
Gloves, 126
Goal-setting, 120, 121
Grasping, 40–41, 51
Grooming for young child,
156–161. *See also* Brushing teeth; Dressing and
undressing; Hair combing
and brushing
Gross motor development.
See Motor development

Hair combing and brushing,
157
Hands
awareness of, 40–41, 45
use for tactile exploration,
186–188. *See also*
Touching
Harness, for teaching
walking, 50
Head raising, 38, 143
Head rolling, 87
Hearing, development of,
65–68, 101–102
"Hide and seek," 134
Hirschberg, Florence, 176
Holding, resistance to, 62
Holidays, preparations and
activities, 179
Household chores, 163–164
Household articles and
furnishings
development of sense of
touch and, 70–71

stability of locations for,
49, 96
as toys, 77, 78, 79–80

Imaginary companion, 142
Imagination, development of,
185–186
Independence, 120–121
191–192
Infancy
importance of verbal
communication in, 31–36
symptoms of other impairments in, 195
Infant feeding, 52–59
drinking from cup, 56–57
finger-feeding, 57–58
and solid foods, 54–55
spoons and, 58–59
Injury, 47
overreaction to, 94
Intellectual development,
language and, 104

Jar opening, 154
Jungle gym, 146
Junior foods, 54

Key, use of, 154
Kiddie car, 134
Kitchen cabinet, exploration
of, 70–71
Knee bends, 39

Lacing, 159–160
Language development
difficult concepts in,
105–106
gaps in, 34, 81

[Language development]
  importance for blind child,
    25, 142-143
  and reading to child, 106
  repetition of words and
    sounds, 33
  in toddler stage, 102-106
  and words indicating space
    and location, 145
  in young child, 141-143
  See also Language use;
    Naming; Verbalization
Language use
  during dressing and
    undressing, 60
  during swimming lessons,
    99
  during trailing, 95
"Leading" child, 149-150
Left-right differentiation, 149
Legal blindness, 23
Lego blocks, 130-131
Light switch box, 100, 133
Light perception, 119-120
  and turning lights on and
    off, 109-110
Location, sound and, 32

Mealtimes
  with family, 55-56
  in toddler stage, 111-113
  for young children,
    160-161
Measures, 174
Memory facilitation, 95,
  182-183
Mobiles, 75-77
Mobility
  outside, 151-152
  and sighted-guide tech-
    nique, 153-154. See also

  Running; Swimming;
    Walking
Monkey bars, 135
Mother, role of, 197
Motivation, for walking, 93
Motor development
  crawling and creeping,
    46-48
  and "doing tricks,"
    144-145
  exercises for, 38-39
  and games teaching space
    and location concepts,
    145
  grasping, 40-41
  and outdoor activities,
    145-146
  reaching, 41-42;
  rolling over, 42-43
  running, 146-147
  sitting, 43-46
  standing and sitting down,
    45-46
  timing and sequence of, 38
  use of sound, 40
  walking independently,
    48-51
  in young child, 144-150
  See also Fine motor
    development
Mourning process, as reaction
  to birth of blind child,
  19
Multiple impairments, 194-
  196
Musical toys, 67

Name, knowledge of, 67-68,
  106
Naming
  body parts, 79, 96
  foods, 113

[Naming]
new experiences, 34
sounds, 68
objects, 33–34, 60, 69,
102–103
people, 102–103. See also
Verbalization
New situations, reaction to,
64
Noise, 66, 102
Numbers. See Counting;
Measures; Sequencing

Object basket, 34, 84–85, 103,
130
Objects
differentiation of attributes
of, 175–176
improvement of sense of
touch with, 69–70
matching, and pre-braille
training 168–170
moving, 32–33
naming, 35, 36, 60
perception of, 92–93
recognition of, 129–130
See also Grasping;
Reaching
Obstacles, perception of, 149,
152–153
Olfactory sense. See Smell
Ophthalmologist, detection of
severely limited vision
by, 110
Orientation learning, 147–150
Outdoors
experiences in infancy, 71
fenced in are for, 134
play, 145–146
play equipment, 135
Overstimulation, avoidance
of, 142

Painting, 187–188
Pantomime, 185–186
Parent-child bond, in toddler
stage, 118–119. See also
Social development
Parents
blindfolding selves, 83–84
and failure to walk, 49–50
reaction to blind child,
19–22, 25–27
separation from, 61–62
See also Family
Parks and playgrounds, 135.
See also Outdoors
Paste, homemade, for
painting, 188
Pegboard, for pre-braille
training, 166–168
People, distinguishing between, sense of smell
and, 109. See also
Strangers
Perception of world, blind
and sighted toddlers
compared in, 91–92
Pets, caring for, 180
Piggy-back rides, 79
Planting, 179–180
Plasticine, 188
Plate throwing, 58
Play
ball-playing, 132–133
with blocks, 183
body contact games, 78–79
fingerpainting, 187–188
imagination and, 185–186
importance in infancy, 74
and interlocking toys,
130–131
and mobiles, 75–77
with music, 135
necessity of intervention
for, 128–129

[Play]
  and objects; *see* Objects
  on outdoor equipment, 135,
    145–146
  outdoors, 134
  pouring, 136
  and tricycles, 137–138
  with water, 134–135
  of young child, 142
  See also Cooking; Games;
    Planting; Toys;
    Woodworking
Playdough, 188
  learning to cut with, 162
Playpen, 43
Popping corn, 184
Posture
  head drooping, 86
  stiff-legged walking, 50
Potty seat, vs. regular toilet
  seat, 116–117
Pouring, 112–113, 136
Pre-braille training, 165–178
  pegboard for, 166–168
  and sorting, 170–173
  and tactile discrimination
    training, 168–173
  See also Counting
Pull-toys, 133
Punishment for blindisms, 87

Radio, television, and record
  players, 65, 67, 135
Reading
  out loud, 106
  readiness, 165–166
  See also Pre-braille training
Record players. *See* Radio,
  television, and record
  players
Resources, 199
Restaurants, 58, 160–161

Ride a Cock Horse, 78–79
Rocking, 87
Roller skating, 146
Rolling over, defining
  boundaries for, 42–43
Running, 96–97, 146–147

Safety
  arms extended forward
    and, 94
  exploration of environment
    and, 70
  of toys, 77–78
Scissors, 182
Sculpting, 188
Seesaw, 135
Self, sense of, 96
Self-care skills. *See* Dressing
  and undressing; Feeding;
  Toilet training
Self-confidence
  independence and, 120–121
  play and, 138
Separation from parents,
  61–62
Sequencing, 174–175
Shoes
  leather soles for, 49
  tying bow, 159–160
Shopping trips, to market,
  184–185
Sighted-guide technique,
  153–154
Sitting, 43–46
Sit-ups, 39
Size differentiation, 129
Sleep
  bowel and bladder control
    during night, 117
  disturbances in infancy,
    72–73
Smell, sense of

[Smell, sense of]
  development of, 71–72,
    108–109, 175
  and language learning, 36
Snap beads, 131
Social development
  and blindisms, 86–87
  and body contact, 62–63
  in infancy, 62–64
  and looking at speaker, 86,
    143
  and reaction to new
    situations, 64
  in toddler stage, 118–120
Solid food
  and chewing as speech
    preparation, 35–36
  introduction of, 54–55
Sorting, in pre-braille
  training, 170–171
Sound
  and crawling and creeping,
    47
  delay in reaching toward,
    41–42
  during infant feeding,
    52–53
  and leather soles, 49
  localization training, 66–67
  matching, 177–178
  motor development and, 40
  naming, 68
  and perception of obstacles,
    152–153
  and toy selection, 133–134
Speech
  muscle readiness for, 35–36
  of parents, 66
Spoon feeding, 58–59, 112
Staircases, 47, 51
Standing, 45–46
Straight line, walking,
  148–149

Strained foods, 53
Strangers, young child's
  reaction to, 141
Street, trips to, 151–152
Swimming, 97–99
Swing, 135
Symptoms, of additional
  impairments, 195–196

Table setting and clearing,
  163–164
Tactile sense
  and barefoot play, 134
  and braille, 166–168
Tactile exploration
  dislike of, 187–188
  improvement of, 186–188
  of store, 185
  in toddler stage, 107–108
  See also Touch
Tactile and auditory mobiles,
  75–77
Talking to oneself, 105
Teething buiscuits, 54
Temperature discrimination,
  174–178
Textures, differentiation
  between, 68–69
Throwing. See Cup throwing;
  Plate throwing
Toddler stage
  discovering severly limited
    vision during, 109–110
  emotional development
    during, 120–122
  fine motor development
    during, 99–100
  language acquisition
    during, 102–106
  mealtimes during, 111–113
  mobility during, 91–100
  play during, 128–138
  of location of toys, 137

[Toddler stage]
  self-care skills during,
    122–127
  social development during,
    118–120
  symptoms of other impair-
    ments in, 195–196
  tactile development during,
    107–108
  toilet training during,
    113–118
Toilet training, 113–118
  emotional development
    and 121
  potty seat for, 116–117
  readiness for, 114–115
Touching
  and counting, 173–176
  during feeding, 37
  improving sense of, 68–71,
    168–173
  and language learning, 36
  and listening skills,
    101–102
  outdoor equipment, 145–
    146
  parents' faces, 63
  and preparation for
    dressing and undressing
    self, 60
  resistance to being held, 62
  speaker's mouth, 103
  and spoon use, 58
  See also Tactile sense;
    Tactile exploration
Tower building, 130
Toys
  age indications on, 83
  blindfolded tryouts of,
    131–132
  choice of, 83–84
  fear of touching, 107–108
  finding, 137

for fine motor coordina-
  tion, 100
interlocking and fitting
  together, 130–131
light switch box, 100
putting away, 136–137
shape and size differentiation in, 129
sound-making, 67
special for blind baby,
  77–78
on wheels, 133
See also Educational toys;
  Musical toys; and under
  individual kinds of, i.e.
  Blocks
Trailing, 95–96, 150–153
Training cups, 56
Travel experiences, 64,
  151–152. See also
  Mobility
Tricks, motor development
  and, 144–145
Tricycles, 137–138
Turning, 147–148

Undressing. See Dressing and
  Undressing
Urination. See Toilet training
Utensils. See Butter knife;
  Fork; Spoon

Verbalizing
  of actions, 60, 113, 119, 135
  of compliments, 124
  of description of outdoor
    play equipment, 145
  description of outings, 186
  of emotions, 143
  of feelings, 121
  importance of, 142–143

Vision, severely limited,
     discovery of, 109–110
Vision-restored adults, 149
Visiting, 119–120, 160–161
Voice tone, during toilet
     training, 117–118
Voices
   new, 120
   selective response to, 64

Walkers, for learning sitting,
     44–45
Walking, 48–51
   environment for, 94–95
   motivation for, 93
   straight line, 148–149
   and trailing method of
     mobility, 95–96
   See also Mobility
Washcloth, use of, 156
Water play, 134–135
Weight, 174, 178
Woodworking, 180–182

Young child
   auditory discrimination

   training, 176–178
fine motor development in,
     154–155
first awareness of own
     blindness, 189–193
grooming, 156–161
household chores, 163–164
language development in,
     141–143
and learning through play,
     179–188
motor development in,
     144–150
need to do for himself,
     141–142
orientation learning, 147–
     150
pre-braille training for,
     165–178
and sighted-guided tech-
     nique, 153–154
symptoms of other impair-
     ments, 196
and trailing method of
     mobility, 150–153
use of hands for tactile
     exploration, 186–188

Zipping, 159–160